God Speaks Through Hurricanes

God Speaks Through Hurricanes

The biblical truth about the weather, global warming and natural disasters

Daniel Harrison

Published by

RICKFORDS HILL PUBLISHING LTD.

P.O. Box 576, Aylesbury, Buckinghamshire HP22 6XX, UK.

First published 2009

ISBN 978-1-905044-16-0

Printed and bound in China by 1010 Printing International Ltd.

Contents

Introduction

– Who Controls the Weather?

As an open-air preacher, my work is very much affected by the weather. Whilst it is not impossible to preach in the rain, the work is certainly hampered. Few people will venture outside and even fewer are willing to stop and talk. Yet over the years, rarely have I been prevented from preaching because of the weather. Many times when it has been raining it has stopped as I've arrived. Equally, I have frequently known it to start raining just when I am packing up to go.

Just recently it had been raining rather heavily all morning and I had prayed that it would stop so that I could go to my local town and preach. Finally the rain cleared. By the time I had driven to the end of my road it had begun raining again. I determined to carry on, but as I drove the five miles to the town where I would be preaching the rain simply got heavier and heavier. I was considering seriously whether I should drive home. Instead I went into a car-park and by the time I had parked the rain had completely stopped. God had certainly answered my prayers. He had shown in a wonderful and obvious way that he controls the elements.

Some time ago a march by Muslims was planned in

my local town. It was designed to focus people on Islam. Concerned by this, a number of local Christians gathered to pray on the day, seeking the face of the Lord that he might intervene and stop it. Just before the march was due to start, the town had torrential rain. As a result, the march was called off and once again God had answered the prayers of his people. Interestingly, most of the surrounding area didn't have any rain.

These are two examples of God controlling the elements. But does God control the weather at all times? Did Hurricane Katrina that wrought devastation in New Orleans in 2005 really come about at God's command? Was the Ethiopian Famine of the mid-1980s the work of God?

In the course of this book we will look at both of these calamities, and many more, asking whether storms and droughts and other weather disasters come about at God's command. We will examine closely what the Bible has to say about droughts, storms and floods. Although we will focus on the weather, we will also deal with earthquakes, principally because they are just as perplexing to people when viewed in the light of an all-powerful God. We will look at events in recent history and attempt to answer that most challenging of questions: Why? The book will also consider, in the light of Scripture, the claim of the majority of scientists that man is causing the earth's climate to change through carbon emissions.

Finally, we will look at how we as Christians should respond to the overarching message of this book, that God uses the weather both in judgment and in mercy.

Biblical basis

Before going any further, I want to make a statement that underpins everything that is written in this book. I believe completely in the authority of the written word of God. Therefore, if I find statements from scientists disagreeing with what the Bible says I consider that the scientists are in error. This might seem a simplistic approach. This might even be seen as naive. However, if we believe the Bible to be the word of God we must stand fully on what it says rather than the words of men. We must remember scientists are merely humans and scientific ideas are only the works of men. It is with this in mind that we shall begin by focusing on the one who created the heavens and the earth.

1

God and His Creation

God as creator and sustainer

When you look up into the vast expanse of sky on a starry night, when you gaze across the wide open sea, or feel the heat of the sun beating down or the full force of a gale, how do you respond?

The word of God declares that all things have been created by God: the sky, the stars, the sea, the sun, the wind – each is the work of his creative hand.

> [He] that liveth for ever and ever... created heaven, and the things that therein are, and the earth, and the things that therein are, and the sea, and the things which are therein (Revelation 10:6).

As we consider all of creation, we should turn our eyes towards the Lord and worship him for creation points to the mercy, power, might, majesty, and glory of God.

> For the invisible things of him from the creation of the world are clearly seen, being understood by the things that are made, even his eternal power and Godhead (Romans 1:20).

In Psalm 136 we have a wonderful exhortation to worship the Lord. The Psalmist urges the congregation to give thanks to the Lord for his mighty works and his mercy. Even God's creation of the heavens, earth, the sun, stars and moon are seen as reflecting his mercy towards us:

> O give thanks to the Lord of lords: for his mercy endureth for ever.
> To him that by wisdom made the heavens: for his mercy endureth for ever.
> To him that stretched out the earth above the waters: for his mercy endureth for ever.
> To him that made great lights: for his mercy endureth for ever:
> The sun to rule by day: for his mercy endureth for ever:
> The moon and stars to rule by night: for his mercy endureth for ever (Psalm 136:3, 5–9).

Ultimately though, everything that was made was created by the hand of God for his pleasure:

> Thou art worthy, O Lord, to receive glory and honour and power: for thou hast created all things, and for thy pleasure they are and were created (Revelation 4:11).

The Letter to the Hebrews, however, goes beyond merely attributing the creation of the heavens and the earth to God. It reveals to us that God, in the person of Jesus Christ, is also sustaining the world, for it is the Son who is 'upholding all things by the word of his power' (Hebrews 1:3).

This is something that should make us stop and think, for it is in effect saying that the only reason why the earth is here today, spinning on its axis, is because of Christ. Without Christ, the universe would not have come into existence and simply would not exist now. We may speak of laws of physics, of gravitational pull, of all these things, but the world does not continue to exist simply because of natural laws but because of Christ's sustaining hand. Moreover, the Letter to the Hebrews goes on to tell us that it is Christ who will bring his creation to an end, when he folds it up like a garment and ushers in the new heavens and the new earth:

> And, thou, LORD, in the beginning hast laid the foundation of the earth; and the heavens are the works of thine hands: they shall perish; but thou remainest; and they all shall wax old as doth a garment; and as a vesture shalt thou fold them up, and they shall be changed (Hebrews 1:10–12).

From the various passages of Scripture already quoted, two important points may be made. First, since it is God who created, and now sustains the world, we can be sure that God continues to care for the world. Without God sustaining the world we could not have any confidence that the world would continue spinning at just the right distance from the sun and at just the right speed. What has happened in the past and what is happening in the present would be no guarantee of the future. However, God has not created the world and then left it to its own devices. We live in a world that God has promised to sustain continuously.

Second, we can assert that nothing can destroy our planet or the universe, and nothing can cause the universe to cease to exist, except God. The reason is that the word of God declares that it is Christ himself who will bring an end to the world. We may see calamities, disasters on a massive scale, but we can be confident of this, that Christ Jesus will bring the world to an end at the appointed time, and not before. He will then bring into being the new heavens and the new earth.

This is essential to our understanding of God's relationship with his creation. He is actively involved in the whole of creation moment by moment. Nothing that is alive would be alive were it not for the sustaining power of Christ. God is sovereign over all and is Lord over all creation.

For the person who acknowledges God as Creator and Lord this means that he is able to rest safe in the knowledge that no calamity, no meteorite and no tsunami can utterly destroy the earth. God is on his throne and is at this very moment intervening in his creation with care, love, mercy, justice and judgment.

2

The God who Controls the Weather

Most, if not all, Christians would agree that at times God intervenes and sends rain, sunshine, storms, wind and various other climatic events. The fact that we pray for fine weather, or for rain in times of drought, surely demonstrates our belief that God does intervene in the natural world. However, how many of us believe that God actively controls the weather at *all* times? That is to say, does God merely intervene from time to time in order that his purposes might be fulfilled or is he constantly commanding the elements to do his bidding and are they continuously responding in obedience? As we search the Scriptures we find that the weather is not a 'natural' phenomenon, but rather something that is subject to the wisdom, power and command of God at all times.

Psalm 107 contains these words:

> For [God] commandeth, and raiseth the stormy wind, which lifteth up the waves thereof… He maketh the storm a calm, so that the waves thereof are still (Psalm 107:25, 29).

From this we understand that it is God who commands

the *stormy wind*. The picture painted here is of the wind waiting for God to utter the command. The moment he does so it acts and causes the waves to rise up. Yet just as it is God who stirs up the *stormy wind* so it is God who causes the wind to be calm. The writer of Proverbs asks, 'Who hath ascended up into heaven, or descended? Who hath gathered the wind in his fists?' When he goes on to ask 'what is his name, and what is his son's name, if thou canst tell?' (Proverbs 30:4), the clear implication is that it is God who has done this. The wind is his creation, it belongs to him for he 'causeth his wind to blow' (Psalm 147:18), and he 'bringeth forth the wind out of his treasures' (Jeremiah 10:13). Yet God not only sends the wind but also, by way of his messengers, holds it back from the earth:

> And after these things I saw four angels standing on the four corners of the earth, holding the four winds of the earth, that the wind should not blow on the earth, nor on the sea, nor on any tree (Revelation 7:1).

When we see the wind blowing with all its might our response should not be to think how great are the forces of nature. Instead, our gaze should be turned to the God who created the wind, who commands it, raises it up and causes it to be still.

In Jeremiah the question is asked, who can cause it to rain?

> Are there any among the vanities of the Gentiles that can cause rain? or can the heavens give showers? Art not thou he, O LORD our God? Therefore we will wait upon thee: for thou hast made all these things (Jeremiah 14:22).

Here we see that the heavens do not have the power to *give showers*. This is further proof that the weather is not a 'natural phenomenon.' Far from being the heavens that are the cause of the rain, it is God himself who causes it to rain upon the earth, for it goes on to say, 'Thou hast made all these things.'

Not only does the Lord send forth the rain – he also withholds it. The Bible makes clear, time and again, that it is God who brings drought and famine:

> This is the thing which I have spoken unto Pharaoh: what God is about to do he sheweth unto Pharaoh. Behold, there come seven years of great plenty throughout all the land of Egypt: and there shall arise after them seven years of famine... And for that the dream was doubled unto Pharaoh twice; it is because the thing is established by God, and God will shortly bring it to pass (Genesis 41:23, 32).

> Then there was a famine in the days of David three years, year after year; and David enquired of the Lord. And the Lord answered, It is for Saul, and for his bloody house, because he slew the Gibeonites (II Samuel 21:1).

> And I called for a drought upon the land, and upon the mountains, and upon the corn, and upon the new wine, and upon the oil, and upon that which the ground bringeth forth, and upon men, and upon cattle, and upon all the labour of the hands (Haggai 1:11).

Just as we experience rain and drought we also know how in the space of a few hours frost or snow can transform the landscape. The water which once flowed freely becomes solid. Why does this happen? What is the cause? Science can explain many things and it may be able to point us to secondary causes. Yet the Bible tells us that it is God who sends the frost, the snow and the ice.

> For he saith to the snow, Be thou on the earth (Job 37:6).
> By the breath of God frost is given: and the breadth of the waters is straitened (Job 37:10).
> Out of whose womb came the ice? and the hoary frost of heaven, who hath gendered it? (Job 38:29).
> He casteth forth his ice like morsels: who can stand before his cold? (Psalm 147:17).

Notice it is his cold – it belongs to God: he created it and he sends it upon the earth. Why does the snow fall upon the earth? Because the Lord commands it. Why does the frost cover the earth? Because it comes by way of the breath of God.

Water vapour, the clouds, hail, thunder and lightning all act at the command of the sovereign, almighty God. They are subject to him and him alone. The Bible could not be clearer in showing this to be the case:

> He directeth... his lightning unto the ends of the earth (Job 37:3).
> He causeth the vapours to ascend from the ends of the earth (Jeremiah 10:13).
> With clouds he covereth the light; and commandeth it not to shine by the cloud that cometh betwixt (Job 36:32).

> He maketh lightnings for the rain; he bringeth the wind out of his treasuries (Psalm 135:7).
>
> He causeth his wind to blow, and the waters flow (Psalm 147:18).
>
> For, lo, he that formeth the mountains, and createth the wind, and declareth unto man what is his thought, that maketh the morning darkness, and treadeth upon the high places of the earth, the LORD, the God of hosts, is his name (Amos 4:13).
>
> The LORD hath his way in the whirlwind and in the storm (Nahum 1:3).
>
> When he made a decree for the rain, and a way for the lightning of the thunder (Job 28:26).
>
> Fire, and hail; snow, and vapour; stormy wind fulfilling his word (Psalm 148:8).

All the elements are under the control and dominion of God. Each responds to his word and executes his purposes. God even controls the earth's relationship with the sun.

On one occasion we find God causing the sun to move back ten degrees. The context of this is when Isaiah goes to Hezekiah telling him to set his house in order for he is about to die. Hezekiah repents and is promised by the Lord that he will be given another fifteen years. He then requests a sign that he will continue to live. He is offered the choice between the sun going backwards or forwards. He chooses that it should go backwards which the Lord brings about in response to Hezekiah's prayer (II Kings 20:9–11).

It might easily be argued that this is merely an example of God stepping in and upsetting the natural order.

However, the Bible makes it plain that our everyday

experience of the sun is determined by God. Matthew tells us that God

> maketh his sun to rise on the evil and on the good, and sendeth rain on the just and on the unjust (Matthew 5:45).

Furthermore, in Genesis 8 we read that God has made a covenant which extends to all mankind:

> While the earth remaineth, seedtime and harvest, and cold and heat, and summer and winter, and day and night shall not cease (Genesis 8:22).

Is it not true that seedtime, harvest, heat, summer and day are all dependent upon the sun for their existence? God has made a promise that these will continue and therefore the sun will continue to rise and set. The idea of the sun rising and setting is a figure of speech that even today's weather forecasters use. We know that the sun does not literally rise and set, but rather the movement of the earth makes it appear that way. However, we should understand from these passages of Scripture that God is constantly commanding the earth to spin on its axis so that we continue to experience day and night and the seasons.

God is sovereign and nothing is outside of his control. The Bible testifies to the fact that it is he alone who controls all weather.

3

God Curses the Earth

God and natural disasters

How many Christians have been asked, 'If there is a God, why are there storms, floods, droughts and famines?' I would suggest that most have been asked this at one time or another. However, the non-Christian usually goes on to say, 'Surely God is good and a good God would not allow such things to happen?' This line of argument leads them to the conclusion that God must either be weak, unloving, or simply not there at all. However, this way of thinking betrays a total misunderstanding of the very nature and person of God.

How do we as Christians respond?

Many will have tried to respond to this question by pointing to the Fall of man. The argument is put forward that God began by making a perfect world but because of man's sin the earth is how it is today. Sin entered in and God's creation was never the same again. However, the Bible has a far deeper answer, one that goes to the very heart of our understanding of God and creation.

The reason why the created world is not perfect is because

God cursed the earth. It is true that God would not have cursed the earth had it not been for man's sin, but the fact remains that the thistles and thorns rose up because God cursed the earth. This will have important consequences as we go on. We tend to see the Fall as being the direct cause of the thorns and thistles without God's intervention. Yet, the Bible says these came as a direct result of God's curse upon the earth:

> And unto Adam he said, Because thou hast hearkened unto the voice of thy wife, and hast eaten of the tree, of which I commanded thee, saying, Thou shalt not eat of it: cursed is the ground for thy sake; in sorrow shalt thou eat of it all the days of thy life; thorns also and thistles shall it bring forth to thee… (Genesis 3:17–18a).

Paul, in his Letter to the Romans makes a similar point when he writes:

> The creature (creation) was made subject to vanity, not willingly, but by reason of him who hath subjected the same in hope. Because the creature itself also shall be delivered from the bondage of corruption into the glorious liberty of the children of God. For we know that the whole creation groaneth and travaileth in pain together until now (Romans 8:20–22).

With regard to the phrase, *subject to vanity*, Dr. Martyn Lloyd-Jones gives a very helpful explanation. 'It means "something which is not fulfilling its function", something which does not measure up to that for which it was intended.'[1] Furthermore, we are told that creation is in *bondage to corruption*. That is to say, death and decay is creation's present lot while it waits to be liberated.

It was God who made creation *subject to vanity* for it was done *in hope*. It was the active work of God. Certainly God would never have subjected creation to *vanity* and to the *bondage of corruption* if it had not been for man's sin; however, it was still God's work to do.

Therefore, from the beginning we find God judging sin by cursing the created world. It is for this reason that creation groans and travails in pain. Furthermore, creation's groaning is made that much worse as God judges creation in response to the ongoing disobedience of mankind. The groaning of creation is directly related to the sin of mankind and her restoration to the glorification of those who have put their trust in Christ.

If we want further proof that the presence of storms, tsunamis, floods and the like are not the natural consequence of the Fall we need look no further than the Flood out of which God saved Noah and his family. Genesis states that before the Flood *there went up a mist from the earth, and watered the whole face of the ground* (Genesis 2:6). What is more, we are told that the rivers and streams watered the plants. There is, however, no mention of rain before the Flood. This leads us to the logical conclusion that it did not rain prior to the Flood. This would surely suggest that though God had judged mankind for his sin by cursing the earth, the original curse had not affected the weather. The weather we experience today is not the inevitable consequence of the Fall because for a number of years the world went on without even knowing any rain let alone floods and droughts. It took another curse from God, the Flood, for the weather to be affected:

And the LORD said, I will destroy man whom I have created from the face of the earth; both man, and beast, and the creeping thing, and the fowls of the air, for it repenteth me that I have made them. ...In the six hundredth year of Noah's life, in the second month, the seventeenth day of the month, the same day were all the fountains of the great deep broken up, and the windows of heaven were opened. And the rain was upon the earth forty days and forty nights. ...And the LORD said in his heart, I will not again curse the ground any more for man's sake (Genesis 6:7; 7:11–12; 8:21).

The Flood is the first occasion in which God uses weather to bring judgment. In direct response to the evil that comes up to him from the earth, God brings judgment:

And God saw that the wickedness of man was great in the earth, and that every imagination of the thoughts of his heart was only evil continually. ...And God said unto Noah, The end of all flesh is come before me; for the earth is filled with violence through them; and, behold, I will destroy them with the earth (Genesis 6:5, 13).

However, simultaneously we see the mercy of God in that he promises never again to curse the whole earth:

And the LORD said in his heart, I will not again curse the ground any more for man's sake; for the imagination of man's heart is evil from his youth; neither will I again smite any more every thing living, as I have done (Genesis 8:21).

The significance of the early chapters of Genesis is that from the beginning of creation human sin led to God's direct intervention in judgment. He cursed the earth in response to man's (specifically Adam's) initial sin, and he cursed the ground and broke open the heavens in response to man's wickedness. Far from being an inevitable consequence of sin, the chaos that resulted can be directly attributed to God's acting in response to man's rebellion.

4

God and the Nations

When one thinks of all the people that live in any particular nation, to suggest that God brings blessings or calamities upon a whole nation might seem indiscriminate and unfair. Surely within any nation at any one time there must be a mixture of both righteous and wicked. However, as we shall see, although God considers every individual separately, on another level he deals with people as a group. Thus it is possible to speak of a righteous nation and a wicked nation, just as it is possible to speak of a righteous or a wicked individual.

Before going on to look at why and how God blesses and judges the nations, we must first consider the relationship God has with the nations. In the Acts of the Apostles, Paul declares that God

> hath made of one blood all nations of men for to dwell on all the face of the earth, and hath determined the times before appointed, and the bounds of their habitation; that they should seek the Lord, if haply they might feel after him, and find him, though he be not far from every one of us... (Acts 17:26–27).

From this we discover four important things about the nations and God's relationship with them. First, it is God who created the nations. Out of one people – *of one blood* – God divided the nations across the whole earth. Second, we discover that the times for each nation have also been decreed by God. Nations rise and fall at God's decree. In the book of Job we find Job declaring that God 'increaseth the nations, and destroyeth them: He enlargeth the nations, and straiteneth them again' (Job 12:23). God rules over everything and that includes the nations. The nations are a testimony to God's intervention in the world in every age, for every generation has known the rising and falling of nations. Calvin observed that:

> Paul doth attribute to God not only a bare foreknowledge and cold speculation, as some men do indiscreetly, but he placeth the cause of those things which fall out, in his counsel and beck. For he saith not that the times were only foreseen, but that they were appointed and set in such order as pleased him best. And when he addeth also that God had appointed from the beginning those things which he had appointed before, his meaning is, that he executeth by the power of his Spirit those things which he hath decreed in his counsel according to that: "Our God is in heaven; he hath done whatsoever he would" (Psalm 115:3).[2]

Third, we find that the geographical size of the nation is determined by God. The boundaries of the nations have been set in place by God's almighty hand.

> [God] hath made of one blood all nations of men for to dwell on all the face of the earth, and hath determined the times before appointed, and the bounds of their habitation (Acts 17:26).

Finally, we find the mysterious purpose of God in forming the nations. Paul writes that the reason why God created the nations was that the people 'should seek the Lord, if haply they might feel after him, and find him, though he be not far from every one of us'(Acts 17:27). F. F. Bruce, asks,

> What was God's purpose in thus arranging time and place so providentially for men and women's well-being? It was, says Paul, in order that they might seek God and find him. Ever since the creation, he says in Rom. 1:20, the things that God has made have pointed clearly to "his everlasting power and divinity".[3]

The implication is that just as creation points to God since it testifies to his power and majesty, so the nations point to God's sovereignty and power.

Not just the individual

In our modern, western worldview, we see everything in terms of the individual. However, for the Jew this would not have been the case. He would have seen beyond simply the individual, and take account of the family, the community and the nation. It is our western mindset that causes us to fail to appreciate the place the nations have in God's economy.

However, this really shouldn't be the case, for there are a number of prominent verses relating to the nations that we know well, though we probably fail really to think about them. Consider the wonderful covenant made by God with Abraham (Genesis 18:18). As a result of the covenant God declares that the nations will be blessed through Abraham. Notice that it does not say individuals in a particular place or even across the whole world. That is what the western mind would expect. Instead, it says the nations will be blessed through Abraham. It is important to note that the word for nations does not simply mean Gentiles. If that were the case, when it says that God will make Abraham into a great nation, we would have to conclude that Abraham was to be made into a Gentile.

When we turn to the New Testament we see further examples of the emphasis being placed on nations rather than the individual. Jesus' last words to his disciples are, 'Go ye therefore, and teach all nations, baptizing them in the name of the Father, and of the Son, and of the Holy Ghost' (Matthew 28:19). Surely we are to teach individuals, but here again we see God addressing the nations. As we move on to the fulfilment of Scripture and the end-times we find that before the Lord returns 'the gospel must first be published among all nations'(Mark 13:10). Matthew also makes the link between the return of the Lord and the preaching of the gospel to all nations; 'and this gospel of the kingdom shall be preached in all the world for a witness unto all nations; and then shall the end come' (Matthew 24:14).

When the Lord returns, he will come to receive unto himself those that belong to him. What form will his judgment take? Certainly he will judge every individual:

> It is appointed unto men once to die, but after this the judgment (Hebrews 9:27).

However, it is also apparent that he will judge the nations:

> And out of his mouth goeth a sharp sword, that with it he should smite the nations: and he shall rule them with a rod of iron: and he treadeth the winepress of the fierceness and wrath of Almighty God (Revelation 19:15).

This is the battle of Armageddon that takes place at the end of the age. It is here that the Lord goes out with the saints in battle against the beast, the false prophet, the kings of the nations and the nations.

By contrast, those who have trusted in Christ will one day be gathered by him. The scene will be a glorious sight:

> I beheld, and, lo, a great multitude, which no man could number, of all nations, and kindreds, and people, and tongues, stood before the throne, and before the Lamb, clothed with white robes, and palms in their hands (Revelation 7:9).

We are saved as individuals; each person who would be saved must be born again. However, every nation on earth will be represented. The nations are important. As a result we need to hold in balance both the individual and the nation.

At this stage it might be suggested that when the Bible speaks of nations it does so in a different way from the modern understanding. That is to say, when the Bible refers to nations it is simply speaking of people groups. However, we know this is not the case, for when the Israelites asked for a king, the reason they did so was so that they might be like other nations (I Samuel 8:5). The nations round about were not just a particular people confined to an area of land. They also had a ruler. Therefore we can say that the nations were much the same as modern nations; a group of people with their own land governed by a ruler.

To understand God's relationship with the nations further it will be helpful to look at two examples from the Bible. The first concerns God's use of Assyria. Although God uses Assyria to judge Israel for her wickedness, ultimately, God judges Assyria for her pride and arrogance in suggesting that the defeat of Israel was her own doing:

> O Assyrian, the rod of mine anger, and the staff in their hand is mine indignation. I will send him against an hypocritical nation, and against the people of my wrath will I give him a charge, to take the spoil, and to take the prey, and to tread them down like the mire of the streets.
>
> Howbeit he meaneth not so, neither doth his heart think so; but it is in his heart to destroy and cut off nations not a few... Wherefore it shall come to pass, that when the LORD hath performed his whole work upon mount Zion and on Jerusalem, I will punish the fruit of the stout heart of the king of Assyria, and the glory of his high looks (Isaiah 10:5–7, 12).

This incident shows how God is intimately involved in the life of each nation. It is made explicit that God judges nations for he wields the rod, Assyria, against Israel. It is also significant that he rules over the nations in that he uses the nations (e. g. Assyria) to carry out his purposes. Finally, such was the pride of the king and nation of Assyria that God ultimately destroyed both of them. Assyria, in her boasting, declares that it is she that has 'removed the bounds of the people' (Isaiah 10:13). When we consider the verses found in Job and Acts[4] we see just how deluded and puffed up the nation had become. It is into that context that the words of the Lord come; 'Shall the axe boast itself against him that heweth therewith?' (Isaiah 10:15).

This event helps us to understand God's view of nations. God does not see the people of the world purely as individuals, although obviously he does see them in that way. He also sees them as communities of people joined together by his almighty hand and gathered together into a particular land.

It is in Abraham's conversation with God with regard Sodom and Gomorrah, however, that we see God's willingness to withhold judgment from a land for the sake of a few righteous people. When Abraham pleads for God's mercy upon Sodom and Gomorrah, he finally asks whether God will judge the land if there are just ten righteous people living there. God assures Abraham that he will be merciful if there are just ten righteous people in Sodom. Since God subsequently judges the land for the wickedness that is being perpetrated, the clear implication is that there were not even ten righteous people living there. However, what should amaze us is the idea that God might be merciful to a land or nation for the sake of a handful of righteous people. This clearly demonstrates the fact that though in terms of salvation we are saved as individuals, as nations we may on certain occasions know God withholding judgment even though there are only a handful of righteous people living in the land.

God's word declares that 'righteousness exalteth a nation: but sin is a reproach to any people' (Proverbs 14:34). Moreover, it says that 'by the blessing of the upright the city is exalted: but it is overthrown by the mouth of the wicked' (Proverbs 11:11). This establishes the fact that any nation that acts righteously will be blessed, whilst a nation that rebels against God may only expect judgment. As to what a righteous nation is, we might define it as one where the leaders rule with equity, compassion and justice. The laws will reflect God's word and the nation as a whole will be marked out by virtue. It is certainly true that there is no such thing as a Christian nation; however, a nation can be righteous and godly.

The king as representative of the people

Just as the nation holds a central place in God's schemes, so do the actions of the king or ruler. The reason for this is that the king represents the people. Many times in the Bible it speaks of the king going in and out before the people. King David was particularly praised by the people for this. The image is of a king leading the people out in battle and then leading them back to a place of protection as a shepherd. If the king is the leader of the people, the decisions he makes will have ramifications for the whole nation since he represents the nation. We see a particular example of this in the reigns of Saul and David: 'Then there was a famine in the days of David three years, year after year; and David enquired of the LORD. And the LORD answered, It is for Saul, and for his bloody house, because he slew the Gibeonites' (II Samuel 1:1). It was Saul who was ultimately at fault in leading his men to war. Yet the whole nation suffered famine. This is not an isolated incident in the Bible. The nation of Israel also suffered as a result of David's disobedience in numbering the people (II Samuel 24). Remember too that it was Pharaoh who would not let the Israelites go and worship God in the wilderness. The consequence of one man's actions was that Egypt came under severe judgment. God takes seriously the actions of the one who leads a nation, since that one person is a representative of the people. The actions that the leader takes on behalf of the people will lead to the people either being blessed or judged. This should lead us to pray diligently for those who govern our land.

However, it is important to understand that a nation gets the leadership she deserves. When Israel provoked the Lord by her sin, God responded by moving David to take an action that would bring judgment upon them.

And again the anger of the Lord was kindled against Israel, and he moved David against them to say, Go, number Israel and Judah (II Samuel 24:1).

Why does one city suffer and another escape?

It is certainly true that on occasions a particular city and only that city comes under the judgment of God. That is to say, the whole nation is not being judged because the whole nation is not guilty of sinning.

One particularly clear example of this is the plagues of Egypt when Pharaoh refused to allow the Hebrews to go and worship God. A number of the plagues are said to afflict only the Egyptians, while the Hebrews are protected. Here God does not judge one town and not another, but one people and not another. However, the principle remains the same. One group is judged because of their unrighteousness, the other meanwhile is saved.

However, on other occasions it may be that God is judging a whole nation by afflicting only one city within the nation. In Amos it is recorded how God caused it to rain on one city and not on another:

And I also have given you cleanness of teeth in all your cities, and want of bread in all your places: yet have ye not returned unto me, saith the LORD. And also I have withholden the rain from you, when there were yet three months to the harvest: and I caused it to rain upon one city, and caused it not to rain upon another city: one piece was rained upon, and the piece whereupon it rained not withered. So two or three cities wandered unto one city, to drink water; but they were not satisfied: yet have ye not returned unto me, saith the LORD (Amos 4:6–8).

Here we are told how it is God that has withheld rain. We see God pouring out his judgment upon one city and not on another. However, there is nothing to suggest that one city was righteous and the other unrighteous. In fact, it is made clear that the whole nation was unrighteous. The reason for God's withholding rain from one city and sending rain on another was in order that the people would see that he was God and turn to him.

Even when all this has been said, it is worth remembering the smallness of nations in the sight of God. How easily we become overawed by the might, power and extent of many of the nations. Yet Isaiah declares:

> Behold, the nations are as a drop in a bucket, and are counted as the small dust of the balance: behold, he taketh up the isles as a very little thing… All nations before him are as nothing; and they are counted to him less than nothing, and vanity (Isaiah 40:15–17).

The nations that God first created did not arise by chance; neither did the nations that we see around us today. Every nation, its size and power, is the result of God's decree. Every nation stands under the watchful eye of Almighty God. God is not only concerned with individuals; he is also concerned with nations. God created and creates the nations of the earth. He rules the nations and therefore it should not surprise us when we find that God blesses and curses the nations.

5

God Judges with Weather – Biblical Examples

God in the storm

When we see pictures in the newspaper, or images on the television, of human suffering as a result of the latest tsunami, storm or famine I wonder what our response is. Are we concerned for the people involved? I am sure there are times when we are deeply moved inside. However, do these calamities also lead us to see that God will not be mocked, and that he will not tolerate sin? Instead of asking the familiar question, *Where is God now?*, we should be proclaiming that God is in the storm and in the famine.

The Bible clearly teaches that when calamity strikes, it is an act of God: 'Shall evil befall a city and the Lord hath not done it?' (Amos 3:6). Commenting on this verse Harry Lacey writes; 'In the same way as the other eight questions [Amos 3:3–8] clearly require the answer No, so does this one. The truth conveyed therefore is inescapable: No! Evil cannot befall a city unless the Lord has acted. The force of these rhetorical questions seems therefore to require that all calamity is the direct result of divine action.'[5]

We see this thought echoed in Isaiah 45:

> I form the light, and create darkness: I make peace, and
> create evil [harm]: I the LORD do all these things (Isaiah
> 45:7).

Every weather disaster is brought about by God in order
that his righteous judgment may be seen, and the nation
or individual may turn to him. But doesn't that make God
into an evil monster? Far from it. Through each calamity
we are being pointed to God's purity, justice, holiness, and
his absolute hatred of sin. Yet God's judgment is always
tempered by mercy. God does judge the nations, but the
full force of his wrath is always held back. The words that
God spoke to Noah after the Flood confirm this:

> The LORD said in his heart, I will not again curse the
> ground any more for man's sake; for the imagination of
> man's heart is evil from his youth; neither will I again
> smite any more every thing living, as I have done
> (Genesis 8:21).

The clearest evidence of the fact that God uses the
weather in judgment is found in Deuteronomy 28. Here
we see God describing the curses that will fall upon Israel
if she disobeys him:

> But it shall come to pass, if thou wilt not hearken unto
> the voice of the LORD thy God, to observe to do all his
> commandments and his statutes which I command
> thee this day; that all these curses shall come upon
> thee, and overtake thee: Cursed shalt thou be in the
> city, and cursed shalt thou be in the field. Cursed shall

be thy basket and thy store. Cursed shall be the fruit of thy body, and the fruit of thy land... And thy heaven that is over thy head shall be brass, and the earth that is under thee shall be iron. The LORD shall make the rain of thy land powder and dust: from heaven shall it come down upon thee, until thou be destroyed. Moreover he will bring upon thee all the diseases of Egypt, which thou wast afraid of; and they shall cleave unto thee. Also ... every plague, which is not written in the book of this law, them will the LORD bring upon thee, until thou be destroyed. And ye shall be left few in number, whereas ye were as the stars of heaven for multitude; because thou wouldest not obey the voice of the LORD thy God (Deuteronomy 28:15–18, 23–24, 60–62).

At the beginning of this passage the direct relationship between sin and calamities is established. Failure to do all that God commands will result in the curses listed falling on the people:

But it shall come to pass, if thou wilt not hearken unto the voice of the LORD thy God, to observe to do all his commandments and his statutes which I command thee this day; that all these curses shall come upon thee, and overtake thee…

The chapter then goes on to describe what curses will be sent to a disobedient people. We have quoted only those verses that directly relate to the weather. Notice how the curses include famine, drought, the plagues of Egypt (including hail and thunder) and *every plague which is not written in the book of the law.*

Solomon dedicates the temple

It was Solomon who had the wonderful privilege of building the temple. Following the completion of the temple, Solomon made supplication to the Lord and part of his prayer was this:

> When heaven is shut up, and there is no rain, because they have sinned against thee; if they pray… and turn from their sin, when thou afflictest them: Then hear thou in heaven… and give rain (I Kings 8:35–36 c.f. II Chronicles 6:26–27).

In this prayer, Solomon acknowledges that God chastens his people and that, in part, he does so by means of the weather. Significantly, God accepts Solomon's prayer, making it clear that there is a relationship between sin and the weather. This further establishes what we have found to be the case in Deuteronomy 28.

At this point it might be suggested that the Bible only establishes a relationship between the sins of Israel and judgment. However, as we shall see, the Bible gives examples of a number of nations being judged by the weather.

Let us look at some biblical examples of God judging with the weather.

Drought and famine

We have already found that it is God who brings drought:

> Thy heaven that is over thy head shall be brass, and the earth that is under thee shall be iron. The LORD shall make the rain of thy land powder and dust: from heaven shall it come down upon thee, until thou be destroyed (Deuteronomy 28:23–24).

The heaven as brass describes the total absence of rain, whilst the earth as iron gives a dreadful image of a land that has not had rain for a long time. Instead of rain there is only *powder and dust*. It is the Lord who does this for it says, *the Lord shall make the rain of thy land powder and dust*.

Closely associated with drought is famine. Again, we see it is the Lord who brings famine:

> Cursed shalt thou be in the city, and cursed shalt thou be in the field. Cursed shall be thy basket and thy store. Cursed shall be the fruit of thy body, and the fruit of thy land… (Deuteronomy 28:16–18a).

In the following examples we will see how drought and famine are sent by God in response to the sins of the nation.

Ruth and the time of the judges

One of the most wonderful stories in the Bible is the account of Ruth and how she was redeemed by Boaz. However, the story begins with Ruth and Naomi her mother-in-law returning to the land of Israel. Naomi had previously departed to Moab with her husband as a result of a famine that ravaged the land. Now, as she returns, her husband and sons are dead. Her return comes about because God has once more blessed the land of Israel and there is grain in the land. However, what had caused God's judgment to come upon the land in the first place? We get the answer to this in the very first verse of the book:

> Now it came to pass in the days when the judges ruled, that there was a famine in the land (Ruth 1:1).

Time and again it is recorded in the Book of the Judges that 'in those days there was no king in Israel: every man did that which was right in his own eyes' (Judges 21:25). The people rejected God's commandments and worshipped idols. It is into this context that the famine that is mentioned at the opening of the Book of Ruth comes. As a result of the rebellion of the children of Israel, God afflicted them with a famine. As to why the Lord brought the famine to an end, the Scriptures do not tell us. However, what we do know is that it was the Lord who caused the land to be fruitful once more:

> [Naomi] arose with her daughters in law, that she might return from the country of Moab: for she had heard in the country of Moab how that the LORD had visited his people in giving them bread (Ruth 1:6).

Haggai

At the beginning of Haggai we find the Israelites have returned from exile in Babylon. They have begun work on rebuilding the temple. However, the people soon become concerned with their own houses rather than the house of God. The word of the Lord comes by way of the prophet Haggai, 'Is it time for you, O ye, to dwell in your ceiled houses, and this house lie waste?' (Haggai 1:4). God, in response to the people's failure to honour him, calls for a drought upon the land.

We are told that 'the heaven over [them] is stayed from dew, and the earth is stayed from her fruit' (Haggai 1:10). What is more, it is God who 'called for a drought upon the land, and upon the mountains, and upon the corn, and upon the new wine, and upon the oil, and upon that which the ground bringeth forth, and upon men, and upon cattle, and upon all the labour of the hands' (Haggai 1:10–11). The judgment covered the whole land and affected every part of their lives. Matthew Henry comments:

> They neglected the building of God's house, and put that off, that they might have time and money for their secular affairs... Now, that the punishment might answer to the sin, God by his providence kept them still behind-hand, and that poverty which they thought to prevent by not building the temple God brought upon them for not building it. They were sensible of the smart of the judgment, and every one complained of the unseasonable weather, the great losses they sustained in their corn and cattle, and the decay of trade; but they were not sensible of the cause of the judgment, and the ground of God's controversy with them. ...God will make us sensible of our necessary and constant dependence upon him, throughout all the links in the chain of second causes, from first to last; so that we can at no time say, "Now we have no further occasion for God and his providence."[6]

As Matthew Henry says, the sin of the people was their concern for their own things rather than the things of God. As a result, the punishment fitted the sin, not in the sense of its extent but in the fact that it hurt the people in the area of their sin and was the very thing necessary to bring the people back to God.

Elijah and the drought

Turning to the life of Elijah we find him on a certain occasion prophesying to Ahab, the king of Israel:

> As the LORD God of Israel liveth, before whom I stand, there shall not be dew nor rain these years, but according to my word (I Kings 17:1).[7]

The reason for the rain being withheld and the consequent famine was that the king had forsaken God's commandments and followed Baalim instead (I Kings 18:18). The nation, represented by the king, had turned from the Lord. Her trust was now in false gods, in Baalim, and so the true living God judged her land. In so doing, God demonstrated his justice, but more than that, showed that the people were dependent upon him for all things. In a later chapter we will return to this event to see why God, in due course, blessed the land of Israel with rain, causing it to bear fruit.

Joseph and the famine throughout the world

Early in the history of the Hebrews we find a famine occurring that spread throughout Canaan and Egypt:

> And the seven years of plenteousness, that was in the land of Egypt, were ended. And the seven years of dearth began to come, according as Joseph had said: and the dearth was in all lands; but in all the land of Egypt there was bread. ...And the famine was over all the face of the earth: And Joseph opened all the storehouses, and sold unto the Egyptians; and the famine waxed sore in the land of Egypt. And all countries came into Egypt to Joseph for to buy corn; because that the famine was so sore in all lands (Genesis 41:53–54, 56–57).

The occasion was while Joseph was in Egypt. We tend to focus on the way God preserved the Hebrews in the midst of the famine. God certainly did do this. However, I wonder if you have ever asked why God brought about that famine in the first place. The Bible answers that question for us. In the Psalms we are told that God broke the 'staff of bread' and the reason was because the people touched the Lord's anointed:

> He [God] suffered no man to do them (the Israelites) wrong: yea, he reproved kings for their sakes; saying, touch not mine anointed, and do my prophets no harm. Moreover he called for a famine upon the land: he brake the whole staff of bread. He sent a man before them, even Joseph, who was sold for a servant: whose feet they hurt with fetters: he was laid in irons: until the time that his word came: the word of the LORD tried him (Psalm 105:14–19).

Joseph was the Lord's anointed and his brothers touched him (persecuted him) when they threw him into a pit and subsequently sold him. The Egyptians touched him when they put him into prison. The result was that the Lord broke the 'whole staff of bread', which is to say, he sent a famine. One of the messages of the Bible is that we should not attack God's people: 'Touch not mine anointed, and do my prophets no harm' (I Chronicles 16:22). When we do, whether they are Jews or Christians, we are attacking God's people. The consequence for a nation is that she can only expect fearful judgment, which is sent so that she wakes up to see the seriousness of her sins.

Saul's bloody house

During the reign of David there was a famine that lasted three years:

> Then there was a famine in the days of David three years, year after year; and David enquired of the LORD. And the LORD answered, It is for Saul, and for

his bloody house, because he slew the Gibeonites (II Samuel 21:1).

Under Saul, Israel had entered into a covenant with the Gibeonites, the result of which meant that Israel promised to protect this people. Thus they became bound to Israel. Matthew Henry, commenting on this passage, writes: 'that which made this an exceedingly sinful sin was that [Saul] not only shed innocent blood, but therein violated the solemn oath by which the nation was bound to protect them.'[8]

Israel had persecuted a people that were now intimately tied to them. Certainly they were not God's chosen people, however, they were bound up with his chosen people. It would seem as though because of the tie that existed, God counted any attack on the Gibeonites as an attack on his own people.

The prophecy of Agabus
In the Book of Acts it is recorded how Agabus foretold a famine that would afflict Jerusalem (Acts 11:28). Although the Bible does not give us a reason for the famine Harry Lacey makes the interesting observation that it occurred in the days of Claudius Caesar (A.D. 45). He writes; 'it seems significant that, after promise of better conduct than some of his predecessors, Claudius Caesar sank to a degradation worse than many of them.'[9]

The relationship between famine and the sword
Before we close this section on famine, it is necessary to make mention of how, on occasions, the Lord sends both famine and war in order to judge a nation. We might think that the sword (or war) is the natural consequence of the

Fall and the sinful nature of man. Indeed, much like other suffering, when questioned about the causes of war, most Christians would probably point the questioner to the sinfulness of human nature. However, this only gives part of the answer. The Bible makes it clear that war is also God's means of judging the nations.

Is it not true that God uses one nation to attack another nation when they have behaved wickedly? We have already seen how God wielded the axe, which was Assyria, against Israel because of her sin (Isaiah 10:5). Similarly we find Babylon coming against Judah because of the sins of Manasseh (Jeremiah 25:9). In due course Babylon comes against the surrounding peoples and nations – Amorites, Moab, Edom, Philistines, Tyre and Egypt (Ezekiel 25).

However, there are times when God judges a land with the sword and famine together. One clear example of this is found in Ezekiel:

> Son of man, when the land sinneth against me by trespassing grievously, then will I stretch out mine hand upon it, and will break the staff of the bread thereof, and will send famine upon it, and will cut off man and beast from it… I send my four sore judgments… the sword, and the famine, and the noisome beast, and the pestilence… (Ezekiel 14:13, 21).

Here we see God promising to judge the land with not only famine and pestilence, but also the sword. Each is sent in response to the sin of the people. When we look at the nations we may be astonished to see how afflicted some are, suffering famine and war at the same time. We look at the plight of the nations and reason that war stems from poverty which in turn is the result of famine. However, both the sword and famine are weapons of judgment in the hands of Almighty God.

Hail

Perhaps the most obvious occasion in the Bible when God judged a nation with hail occurred when five kings set their armies against Gibeon. Gibeon had previously made peace with Israel. Therefore, the people of Gibeon called on Joshua for help. Many of those who were against Gibeon were slaughtered by Joshua's army. However, greater were the number who were slain as a result of the hailstones that God cast down from heaven:

> And it came to pass, as they fled from before Israel, and were in the going down to Bethhoron, that the LORD cast down great stones from heaven upon them unto Azekah, and they died: they were more which died with hailstones than they whom the children of Israel slew with the sword (Joshua 10:11).

We are also told that in the end-times there is to be a great hailstorm:

> And there fell upon men a great hail out of heaven, every stone about the weight of a talent: and men blasphemed God because of the plague of the hail; for the plague thereof was exceeding great (Revelation 16:21).

A talent is about one hundred pounds so it is evident that this will be something the like of which the earth has never previously seen. Significantly, the storm is spoken of in the context of 'the fierceness of (God's) wrath' (Revelation

16:19) and so hail is a demonstration of God's anger against a nation.

Floods

The worldwide flood in the days of Noah was the first example of God using the weather to judge a group of people:

> The earth also was corrupt before God, and the earth was filled with violence. And God looked upon the earth, and, behold, it was corrupt; for all flesh had corrupted his way upon the earth. And God said unto Noah, The end of all flesh is come before me; for the earth is filled with violence through them; and, behold, I will destroy them with the earth (Genesis 6:11–13).

There is a general principle laid out in the word of God that a nation that commits gross wickedness will, but for the mercy of God, experience floods. Floods were one of the judgments that God sent upon Ephraim for her pride:

> Woe to the crown of pride, to the drunkards of Ephraim, whose glorious beauty is a fading flower, which are on the head of the fat valleys of them that are overcome with wine!
> Behold, the LORD hath a mighty and strong one, which as a tempest of hail and a destroying storm, as a flood of mighty waters overflowing, shall cast down to the earth with the hand (Isaiah 28:1–2).

Floods are directly associated with wickedness, by which we mean gross sins. A nation that has cast off all restraints and has allowed and even encouraged awful immorality, should be aware that God's judgment will take the form of floods. When we remember that rain is a picture of God's righteousness, this makes sense since by flooding the nation God is pouring forth his righteous judgment upon the nation. What is more, in sending forth his righteousness it is with the purpose of cleansing the nation from all its wickedness. Although sin could never be removed as a result of a flood, there is a sense in which God 'cleanses' the earth from the wickedness that had been perpetrated.

Thunder

Thunder symbolises the power, might and authority of God. Consider the following verse from I Samuel:

> The adversaries of the Lord shall be broken to pieces; out of heaven shall he thunder upon them: the Lord shall judge the ends of the earth; and he shall give strength unto his king, and exalt the horn of his anointed (I Samuel 2:10).

Compare this with what the Psalmist says:

> The voice of thy thunder was in the heaven: the lightnings lightened the world: the earth trembled and shook (Psalm 77:18).

Four specific examples show how thunder bears witness to God's authority and righteous judgment. First, during the time of Samuel the Philistines came against Israel to destroy them:

> And as Samuel was offering up the burnt offering, the Philistines drew near to battle against Israel: but

the LORD thundered with a great thunder on that day upon the Philistines, and discomfited them; and they were smitten before Israel (I Samuel 7:10).

On another occasion we find Samuel saying to the people:

Is it not wheat harvest today? I will call unto the LORD, and He shall send thunder and rain; that ye may perceive and see that your wickedness is great, which ye have done in the sight of the LORD, in asking you a king. So Samuel called unto the LORD; and the LORD sent thunder and rain that day: and all the people greatly feared the LORD and Samuel (I Samuel 12:17–18).

The context here is the people's desire for a king. Samuel, as a result of their unwillingness to acknowledge God as King, calls upon the Lord to send down thunder and rain. Consequently, the wheat harvest is destroyed. The great sin committed by the people was failure to acknowledge the greatness of the Lord. In asking for a king they were, in effect, saying that an earthly king was greater than God. By sending forth thunder out of the heavens God declared his might, power, and greatness. The people saw God's might and realised their sin.

When God gave the Ten Commandments he spoke forth with thunder and lightning:

...all the people saw the thunderings, and the lightnings, and the noise of the trumpet, and the mountain smoking: and when the people saw it, they removed, and stood afar off. And they said unto Moses, Speak thou with us, and we will hear: but let not God speak with us, lest we die. And Moses said unto the people,

> Fear not: for God is come to prove you, and that his fear may be before your faces, that ye sin not (Exodus 20:18–20).

Finally, because of Pharaoh and the Egyptian's refusal to acknowledge and submit to God, God sent forth thunder. God manifested his power but still Pharaoh refused to submit:

> And Moses stretched forth his rod toward heaven: and the LORD sent thunder and hail, and the fire ran along upon the ground (Exodus 9:23).

When we hear thunder we should consider God's power and strength. When we experience a light thunder storm we should praise God for his mercy since if he were to show all his power and majesty we would be destroyed. When a nation experiences a severe thunder storm that brings destruction it should lead her to repent of rejecting God's authority.

Storms/Wind

In examining the role storms play in the economy of God we need to distinguish between storms which are localized and only affect a very few people, and more widespread storms which affect a large number of people.

Jesus in the boat

On one occasion Jesus got into a boat with his disciples in order to sail across to the other side of the Sea of Galilee. The Bible records that 'there arose a great storm of wind, and the waves beat into the ship, so that it was now full' (Mark 4:37). However, Jesus was asleep. The disciples were afraid and woke him. Immediately, Jesus 'arose, and rebuked the wind, and said unto the sea, Peace, be still. And the wind ceased, and there was a great calm. And he said unto them, Why are ye so fearful? how is it that ye have no faith?' (Mark 4:39–40).

Through this Jesus proved himself to be the Son of God, for as the disciples testified, 'even the wind and the sea obey him' (Mark 4: 41). However, why did that storm arise in the first place? I believe that the Bible gives us a wonderful insight into what was happening when Jesus stilled the storm. Let us remember that when interpreting the Bible, a fundamental rule is that Scripture interprets Scripture. That is to say, if we want to understand one verse or passage we should go to another verse or passage that deals with the same theme. Psalm 107 reveals that it is God who both causes the wind and quietens the wind; 'for he commandeth, and raiseth the stormy wind, which lifteth up the waves thereof... He maketh the storm a calm, so that the waves thereof are still' (Psalm 107:25, 29).

From these two verses, we are able to understand what was happening on the Sea of Galilee. It was Jesus who both caused the storm as well as stilled the storm.

As the disciples were in the boat the whole nation was not coming under the judgment of God. Rather, God was afflicting certain men for a specific reason. I believe that the reason was their unbelief. Indeed, Jesus subsequently rebukes them for their lack of faith. As a result of their failure to trust and to yield to the Lord, Jesus sent a storm. If we find this hard to comprehend then we should remember how important faith is to God. God responds to faith throughout the biblical accounts of man's relationship with him. God always takes seriously unbelief in the hearts of people. Significantly, it should not have escaped the reader's notice that the judgment was appropriate for the sin in question, for in the midst of the storm the disciples cry out to the Lord to save them. The storm was sent to deal with a specific failing in the hearts of the disciples.

Jonah and the storm

When God told Jonah to go to the people of Nineveh with a message calling them to repent, Jonah refused to yield and went instead to Tarshish. As a result of his rebellion, God sent a storm to afflict Jonah. In the midst of the storm, Jonah himself acknowledged that this was the Lord's doing and that it was a result of his own sin.

Just as Jonah knew the reason for the storm, I believe that we can always know the reason for God's judgments. If there was no way of knowing the reason for the judgment there would be no way of repenting. Every judgment of God is to bring a person, a people or a nation back to himself in repentance. If we enquire of God the reason for his judgment he will quickly show us.

Paul shipwrecked

A final example of a localized storm is the one which is recorded at the end of the Book of Acts. Paul, along with a number of other prisoners, is taken under guard to Italy. In the course of their journey 'there arose ... a tempestuous wind, called Euroclydon' (Acts 27:14). The gravity of the situation was such that 'neither sun nor stars in many days appeared, and no small tempest lay on us' (Acts 27:20).

Though the storm was severe and looked as if it would result in much loss of life, God assured Paul that everyone would be saved. The reason for Paul being saved was so that he would testify in Rome. Furthermore, from what is written, it would seem clear that there is a direct connection between Paul's deliverance and that of the rest of the men on board:

> And now I exhort you to be of good cheer: for there shall be no loss of any man's life among you, but of the ship. For there stood by me this night the angel of God, whose I am, and whom I serve, saying, Fear not, Paul; thou must be brought before Caesar: and, lo, God hath given thee all them that sail with thee (Acts 27:22–24).

Here we see the righteousness of one man leading to the deliverance of those who were with him. Paul goes on to say that though they will all be saved; they 'must be cast upon a certain island' (Acts 27:26). The island that they end up on was not any island; it was *a certain* island. In the providence of God the *barbarians* of this island received the Gospel. Certainly many received their physical healing and so it is right to assume that many experienced spiritual healing as well.

We may understand that God in his providence caused Paul to be saved along with the others on board ship. We may recognise God's plan in bringing salvation to the island of Melita. However, we may still be left wondering why such a severe storm was necessary and why were the sun and stars hidden from view? By turning to Paul's thorn in the flesh we find the reason for the storm. Paul was given a thorn to keep him humble and dependent upon the Lord following the visions that he had received. Many have wondered what the thorn was and made suggestions. Yet the Bible tells us clearly. It was 'the messenger of Satan.' It wasn't sickness or any other such thing. It was a demon – that is what a messenger of Satan is. Now what was that demon sent to do? It was sent to buffet him. The buffeting wasn't the thorn, the thorn was the messenger. The buffeting was the consequence of the thorn. We are then told the nature of that buffeting in the following verses:

> And lest I should be exalted above measure through the abundance of the revelations, there was given to me a thorn in the flesh, the messenger of Satan to buffet me... Therefore I take pleasure in infirmities, in reproaches, in necessities, in persecutions, in distresses for Christ's sake: for when I am weak, then am I strong (II Corinthians 12:7, 10).

Paul was buffeted in part by distresses. He mentions elsewhere shipwrecks (II Corinthians 11:25). It would seem as though this shipwreck recorded at the end of the Book of Acts was part of Paul's buffeting. If this is the case then it would mean that this shipwreck was part of God's purpose in keeping Paul humble. Finally, it is important to note that Paul says that *there was given to me a thorn in the flesh*. It was God who was the cause of Paul's thorn in the flesh.

Storms and the nations

When we turn to storms that sweep across a whole nation we find the following principle holds true: those that come against the land of Israel can only expect the whirlwind, which will scatter God's enemies. The prophet Isaiah declared:

> Fear not, thou worm Jacob, and ye men of Israel; I will help thee, saith the LORD, and thy redeemer, the Holy One of Israel. Behold, I will make thee a new sharp threshing instrument having teeth: thou shalt thresh the mountains, and beat them small, and shalt make the hills as chaff. Thou shalt fan them, and the wind

shall carry them away, and the whirlwind shall scatter them: and thou shalt rejoice in the Lord, and shalt glory in the Holy One of Israel (Isaiah 41:14–16).

When we turn to modern day examples of storms, we will see that they are frequently sent by God when a nation attempts to come against the nation of Israel.

God – Not in the wind, earthquake or fire

Although we have established the clear link between climatic disasters and God's judgment, there still remains one passage of Scripture that might, on first reading, seem to call this into question. It is the occasion when God speaks to Elijah in a 'still small voice' (I Kings 19:10–18).

Here we see Elijah bemoaning the fact that he, alone, is left among the prophets. He has proved himself to be faithful to God. Yet now he finds his life under threat. It is for that reason that he hides in a cave. In response to Elijah's words, the Lord tells him to 'stand upon the mount before the Lord' (I Kings 19:11). Elijah is told to go up the mountain in order to see the nature and character of the Lord.

In the light of Elijah's appeal to his own righteousness, and the threat he is under, he expects God to judge the children of Israel and the prophets. When Elijah is taken up the mountain he experiences wind, earthquake and fire. However, he finds that the Lord is not in any of these. Elijah expected the Lord to be in any one, or all, of these, since each one of these would have revealed the judgment of God. Instead, the Lord revealed himself in a *still small voice*. This speaks of the mercy and grace of God. Following this, Elijah returns to the cave. Clearly, having seen that God was not going to judge the people, he went and hid, still fearful for his life.

Again the Lord asks what Elijah is doing there and the prophet gives the same answer as he has given earlier. It is now that we see the grace and mercy of God. The Lord tells Elijah to anoint a king of Syria and a prophet to take Elijah's place. Finally, he tells him that he has reserved seven thousand who have not bowed before Baal. It is for this reason that God was not going to judge the children and prophets of Israel. God did send the wind, the earthquake and the fire, but he did so to show that though he was able to judge he had shown grace to Israel for he was not in any of these. The message of this event in the life of Elijah, is not that there are occasions when weather is not the result of God's judgment or blessing, rather, that God sent these climatic events to show that he was not judging Israel but having mercy on her. It was the Lord's means of showing himself to Elijah.

As we have looked at various climatic calamities recorded in the Bible, we have found each time that they are the work of the Lord. Moreover, we have seen that they have been sent with the purpose of causing the nation to return to God. It is for this reason that we can say that every natural disaster is for our good. Additionally, there is a correlation between the sins of the nation and the judgment that is forthcoming. The nature of the judgment is what is necessary to bring the nation or individual to repentance.

6

The Weather, God's Judgment and Modern History

God's use of the weather in judgment is not confined to the history of Israel and the pages of the Bible. In this chapter we will examine some of the great climatic catastrophes of history.

Spanish Armada

At a certain point in history England found herself subject to the full force of one of the greatest navies of the time. What is more, this navy had as its object the bringing to these shores of Catholicism and with it the overthrow of the Protestant faith. What transpired was one of the most powerful and glorious demonstrations of God's providence. The navy that had launched its attack upon England's shores was literally smashed to pieces and those ships that did manage to limp home were very few in number. In one mighty act of God, England was saved, and the opposing navy was destroyed.

The Spanish Armada sailed forth with the aim of defeating Elizabeth I, replacing her with a Catholic Infanta and spreading Catholicism across the whole of Northern Europe. As Spain's ships approached the shores of England, battle ensued. After a number of days of fighting the English fleet launched burning ships amongst the Spanish Armada.

The Spanish ships had planned to meet up with armies assembled in Dunkirk ready to attack England. Despite the burning ships, the Spanish carried on with the plan, only to find that the armies were not there, the reason for which we will see in due course. The Armada therefore turned around and battle was rejoined. In time both navies ran out of ammunition and the Spanish fled. As they did so they encountered a great storm that swept them onto the rocks off the coasts of Norway and Ireland: hundreds died and a huge number of vessels never made it back.[10] The Spanish Armada, that great fleet, was destroyed in one night – not by the bravery of England's men, or because of their expertise in battle, but because the wind raged and the waves roared. That night all believers would have seen the truth of the Prophet's cry:

> The Lord is slow to anger, and great in power, and will not at all acquit the wicked: the Lord hath his way in the whirlwind and in the storm, and the clouds are the dust of his feet (Nahum 1:3).

Indeed, the nation acknowledged God's protective hand, for a commemorative medal was struck declaring that 'God blew, and they were scattered.'[11] How ironic then that the Spanish left their shores with flags inscribed with the words; 'Arise, Lord, and vindicate your cause.'[12] One Spanish sea-captain said, we sail 'in the confident hope of a miracle', which will send 'some strange freak of weather.'[13]

Yet a previous storm, frequently overlooked, had also been vital to the defeat of the Armada. The plan had been for the Spanish Armada to sail from Spain, and eventually up the Channel, where they would meet the Duke of Parma who was to be positioned at Dunkirk. He and his army would then sail across to England and land under the cover of the Armada. The army would then invade England and set up the Infanta in place of Queen Elizabeth I. And so England would fall prey to the Catholic Spanish Empire.

However, God commanded the winds to blow as soon as the Spanish launched out from Spain and such was the destruction it took two months for the repairs to be carried out. The significance of this was that by the time the Spanish reached the English Channel, England was prepared. More importantly though, when the Armada did meet up with the Duke of Parma the tides were low and he and his army were stuck in port unable to go anywhere. God had commanded the winds and therefore not a single soldier managed to set foot in England.

The defeat of the Spanish Armada saw the blessing of one nation while another was judged. Certainly Christians down the ages have given thanks to the Lord for his blessing of protection on that night. They have been right to do so and it is essential that we remember such events. However, I wonder how many have considered that it was also a moment when God judged a nation for their rejection of his word and for her attempt to spread Catholicism throughout the world. God destroyed the Egyptians who pursued the Israelites while simultaneously delivering the children of Israel. The mercy and judgment of God was married together on both occasions.

Lisbon Earthquake of 1755

On 1st November 1755 something happened that shook the world – literally and metaphorically. An earthquake hit the city of Lisbon in Portugal causing the deaths of as many as 90,000 people. The epicentre of the earthquake was in the Atlantic Ocean and such was its force (estimated to be 9.0 on Richter scale) that tremors were felt as far away as Finland, Northern Italy and North Africa. The earthquake reportedly lasted about five minutes and within those few moments thousands of Lisbon's houses were destroyed, many of her splendid buildings were reduced to rubble and her glory and wealth were no more. The greatest loss of all was the thousands who died. In the wake of the earthquake, fires spread across the city. As the earthquake subsided many of those who had survived ran to the sea for safety. The horror of what they had just seen was now exacerbated. What followed was an enormous tsunami, whose waves flooded the city, taking the lives of many more. The earthquake and the tsunami combined resulted in Lisbon being almost totally destroyed.

All of this had a profound effect upon the people of Europe. It influenced numerous sermons, paintings and writings. Indeed, Voltaire's *Candide* was, at least in part, influenced by the Lisbon Earthquake.

Yet was the Lisbon Earthquake really caused by God? If so why did he judge Lisbon and why was his judgment so severe?

John Wesley produced a sermon entitled, *Serious Thoughts Occasioned by the Late Earthquake at Lisbon*. Here Wesley responds to the charge that such an event is 'purely natural and accidental; the result of natural causes':

> If by affirming, 'All this is purely natural,' you mean, it is not providential, or that God has nothing to do

with it, this is not true, that is, supposing the Bible to be true. For supposing this, you may discant ever so long on the natural causes of murrain, winds, thunder, lightning, and yet you are altogether wide of the mark, you prove nothing at all, unless you can prove, that God never works in or by natural causes. But this you cannot prove, nay none doubt of his so working, who allows the scripture to be of God. ...Therefore, allowing there are natural causes of all these, they are still under the direction of the Lord of nature. Nay, what is nature itself but the art of God? Or God's method of acting in the material world?

...And what shall we say of the late accounts from Portugal? That some thousand houses, and many thousand persons, are no more! That a fair city is now in ruinous heaps! Is there indeed a God that judges the world? And is he now making inquisition for blood? If so, it is not surprising, he should begin there, where so much blood has been poured on the ground like water! Where so many brave men have been murdered, in the most base and cowardly as well as barbarous manner, almost every day, as well as every night, while none regarded or laid it to heart.[14]

To John Wesley, the Lisbon Earthquake was a clear sign of God's justice being meted out against a nation which had sinned grievously against the Lord. Here was a country that was built upon the heresy of Catholicism and had persecuted the Protestants who dwelt there through the Inquisition.

Yet Wesley did not speak with the voice of one who would condemn another nation while excusing the actions of his own. How could he when just five years before England had

had an earthquake of her own, albeit very small? Rather, he called the people of England to repent and get right with God. Here we see echoes of Jesus' words to those who came asking if certain people were worse sinners because they had suffered (Luke 13:1–5).[15] Every earthquake is certainly a manifestation of God's judgment against a nation, something that Wesley propounds. However, we should never lose sight of the fact that another's plight is a warning to us.

The Great English Earthquake

This earthquake occurred on April 22nd 1884 and is the greatest earthquake England has known. Peter Haining in his book on the earthquake writes:

> It sounded like the crack of doom. A low, rumbling noise that built to a terrifying intensity and then caused the ground to oscillate, turning towns, villages and the whole countryside into great waves of movement like a storm-tossed sea. Buildings and churches swayed and crumbled, houses and cottages shook open in explosions of smoke and debris, and in a moment more, a terrified and panic-stricken population took screaming to the streets.[16]

A little later in the book Peter Haining comments on the social setting of the time:

> England, and indeed the whole of the United Kingdom, was enjoying a period of great prosperity and international influence in the 1880s. The famed British Empire 'on which the sun never set' was at its most powerful and far-reaching... In England men

and women in most classes enjoyed affluence and prosperity. Ronald Blythe describes the first effect thus, 'The great Essex earthquake had a remarkable effect upon the materialistic complacency of the age, receiving an astonished press and filling the churches with anxious worshippers who feared that such disturbances followed a serial pattern.'[17]

Peter Haining goes on to say that the earthquake 'also devastated that particular Victorian idyll that anything made of bricks and mortar was somehow sacred. Looking at the acres of ruined mansions, the broken towns and villages, the Victorian of 1884 saw a blow to the very foundations of his beliefs.'[18] This shaking of the complacency and foundations of the English was surely the hand of God and it certainly drove them to God.

The Great Storm
On the 16th October, 1987, Britain experienced the worst storm in her recorded history. Why did it happen? I would point to the fact that at the time Thatcherism had taken hold. For all the good it may have done in some ways, one of the consequences, intended or otherwise, was that greed had gripped the nation. Individuals were pursuing a manic materialistic and hedonistic lifestyle. It was into this situation that God spoke in judgment. He literally shook the nation. Three days after the storm he shook the financial markets, causing share prices to plunge. It is perhaps interesting to note that in March of that same year, the *Herald of Free Enterprise* ferry sank. It was pointed out at the time, and has been since, that the sinking of this particular ferry was no coincidence. God was judging the proclamation of free enterprise. We are to herald the

Gospel, not *free enterprise*. On three occasions God spoke, and each time he came in judgment.

Cape Town – 1994

Since 1859 the Parliamentary sessions in Cape Town had been opened in prayer to the God of the Bible. As Dr. Peter Hammond has observed, 'the first action of the new ANC government in 1994 was to abolish the practice of opening Parliament in prayer. That very month, May 1994, Cape Town was hit with the worst storm in living memory and an ecological disaster as a Chinese oil tanker sank off [South Africa's] shores in that storm.'[19] When God is removed from the life and government of the nation, we can only expect his judgment. The fact that we do not always receive his judgment is a testimony to his mercy and longsuffering rather than to any virtue on the part of the nation concerned.

Basilica of St. Francis – 1997

According to Catholic World News, the 13th-century basilica, built to honor the founder of the Franciscan order, [became] an international symbol of peace and interreligious dialogue after Pope John Paul held multifaith prayer services there in 1986 and 1993.'[20] In 1997 two earthquakes occurred which seriously damaged the Basilica. God was coming against one of the symbols of the ecumenical movement.

Storms in Britain – 2002

On 27th October 2002 seven people were killed as storm force winds raged across Britain. 'Airports and roads were closed, ferry services suspended and power supplies to more than 100,000 homes cut as winds of up to 96mph battered the country, causing damage of at least £50 million.'[21] Significantly, on 16th October 2002 the House of Lords voted in favour of giving homosexual couples the right to adopt. This acted as the last real opportunity for this piece of legislation to be stopped since MPs had already voted in favour of giving homosexuals this right. God's wrath was demonstrated in a very clear way in Britain that year.

Boscastle – 2004

On August 16th 2004 the river flowing through Boscastle burst its banks. It was reported that the surge of water rushed through the high street at forty miles an hour. It resulted in 'the largest peacetime rescue in the history of mainland Britain.'[22] Much damage occurred although miraculously no lives were lost. It was caused by torrential rain, but what was the spiritual reason? As Jane Marshall observed, Boscastle 'has the only witchcraft museum in Britain, holding the world's largest collection.'[23]

Boxing Day Tsunami

Once again the world questioned and searched for an answer, as images were beamed into sitting rooms across the world, of gigantic waves hitting the shores of Indonesia on Boxing Day 2004. Once more the people asked, If there is a God why would he allow something like this to happen?

300,000 people died across twelve countries as an earthquake in the Indian Ocean caused waves as high as 35 metres to sweep against the shores.

Many responded by saying that this was final proof that there was no God. If God is a God of love, he would not allow such a thing, they contended. Yet those who made such remarks were in reality saying that they knew best and that their justice was superior. Above all though, they had failed to see the holiness of God.

It should not surprise us that God judged Indonesia. This country has for a long time persecuted Christians severely, as the following report makes clear. God does not turn his eyes away from such things forever, but upholds his justice in everything he does.

> 'Indonesia is in the process of being destroyed. Our economy has collapsed, thanks to all this foreign meddling. Christians and their co-conspirators like the IMF have created this chaos. The time has come for Islam to fight back.' So said Brigadier General Kastor, a former aide to President Suharto, thereby increasing the public mood of hostility towards Christians who became a scapegoat for the economic chaos in Indonesia and suffered violent attacks.
>
> One result was a campaign of persecution, which began when the first of 7–15,000 armed Islamic militants were sent to the Moluccas to launch an attack against Christians in May 2000. Over 1000 people were butchered in a single raid. In another, 200 were killed and their bodies horribly mutilated. In June some 200 Christians sheltering in a church were attacked with machetes. The church was then set on fire. At least 100 Christians died in the blaze. In another incident three children were tied up and dragged to their death behind a speeding car. At Duma, Halmahera island, 135 people were killed in one attack and nearly 300 Christian women and girls were abducted. They are believed to have been taken to another island where they have been raped. 700 Christians on Ceram Island

were warned that they would be killed if they did not become Muslims. News emerged later that another 5000 Christians on the island had been forced to convert earlier in the year. On Bacan island 1150 Christian men and boys were reported to have been forcibly circumcised (as a sign of conversion to Islam). By December there were approximately 487,000 Christian refugees from the Moluccas. Of these some 300,000 have fled from the Moluccas to other parts of Indonesia, the rest are displaced within the Moluccas region.

On November 15th 2000 Jaffar Umar Thalib, leader of the Laskar Jihad, stated in an interview with two reporters that the time had come to introduce Shari'ah (Islamic law) to the Moluccas. 'We intend during Ramadan to carry out various activities paving the way for full Shari'ah at least in places that have now become exclusively Muslim such as the islands of Ternate, Tidore and Bacan.' The chilling reason these islands have become 100% Muslim is that all their Christian inhabitants have been killed or driven out.[24]

Hurricane Katrina

In 2005 America suffered as a result of a particularly terrible hurricane. New Orleans bore the full brunt, as buildings were ripped up, the city was flooded, and thousands died. When we consider the spiritual state of the area it is not hard to discern that God was speaking in and through the storm. New Orleans is renowned for its decadence and immorality. Indeed, there was to have been an openly homosexual festival at the very time the hurricane hit. God had poured out his fury against a city that had ignored him and rebelled openly against him. However, two things should be remembered in the light of what happened to New Orleans. The first is that God's judgment is always measured by mercy and acts as a call to repentance. Here was God speaking to the people of New Orleans in judgment but his hand was partially withheld for his fury could have been much worse. Second, there was a message for the rest of the world; if we do not turn to the Lord in repentance and supplication we can only expect a similar thing to fall on us.

Floods in Britain

In the summer of 2007 floods hit Britain. Crops were devastated, hundreds of thousands were left without water and many more without electricity. Many were quick to point to a link with climate change. However, there were those who declared that what we were witnessing was a judgment from God. Yet were they right, and if they were, what was the sin that had caused God to pour forth his anger upon the nation?

Only a few months before the floods, the government introduced a piece of legislation entitled *Sexual Orientation Regulations*. As a result it became illegal to discriminate on the grounds of sexual orientation. This meant that bed and breakfast establishments were forced to allow same sex couples to share rooms. Furthermore, adoption agencies were no longer able to discriminate against homosexual couples who wanted to adopt. These were only two of the implications of the new laws, but what was immediately apparent was the consequences for both Christian businesses and charities, as well the moral fabric of the nation.

Floods in Bangladesh, Northern India and Nepal

During 2007 Bangladesh suffered horrendous floods. Northern India and Nepal also suffered greatly. The whole region saw thousands die and millions lose their homes. One witness compared it to the Boxing Day Tsunami. Once more people asked the age-old question, 'Why?'

Open Doors is a Christian organisation that monitors and works with persecuted Christians across the world. In their top fifty worst offending nations, at the time of the floods India was at 29, Bangladesh 44 and Nepal 48.[25] In the light of the link we have established between persecuting God's people and judgment, these statistics are significant. It may be asked why the other nations in the list didn't suffer a similar fate. The reality is, many of the other nations have. Furthermore, as we shall see, when a nation escapes judgment, it is reflective of God's longsuffering and should lead to repentance, for God will not endure the sins of a nation forever.

Burmese Cyclone – 2008

In May 2008 Burma suffered a terrible Cyclone that killed more than 100,000 people. The cyclone hit the rice-growing centre of Burma. Since Burma is a net-exporter of rice, this affected the economy seriously. What was the reason? Burma has a terrible record when it comes to the persecution of Christians. When a nation does something of this sort God's hand is not restrained for ever.

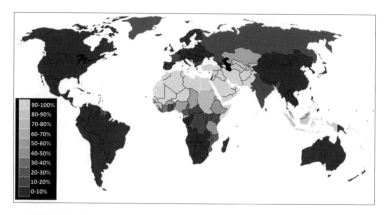

■ Muslim distribution. Data source: *CIA The World Factbook 2008*

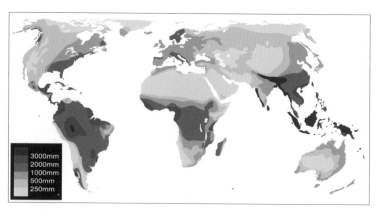

■ World average precipitation. Copyright © 2009 www.mapsofworld.com

7

The Weather, God's Judgment and the Nations

Drought and the Muslim nations

One of the clearest pieces of evidence that weather and God's judgment go hand in hand may be seen by looking at two maps of the world, one showing rainfall distribution and the other showing the proportion of Muslims living in any given place. What is noticeable is how, almost without exception, those countries with the highest Muslim population have the least rainfall. Looking at the map of rainfall we see the northern part of Africa, the Horn of Africa and large parts of Asia afflicted by a serious lack of rainfall. These are the very areas of the globe where Muslims dominate. The fact that many of these countries have systematically persecuted Christians should mean that we are not surprised that God judges these lands. More than that, Muslims are worshipping a false god who, some have suggested, is a fertility god. This being so, the fact that God is seen to judge the land of these Muslim nations, so causing it not to be fertile has added significance. Once more we see an example of the judgment fitting perfectly the sin of the people.

A particular example of God judging the Muslim nations came in the Sahel Famine of 1968–1975. The drought in due course devastated Mauritania, Senegal, Mali, Niger, Chad, Sudan, Ethiopia, Somalia, Gambia, parts of Tanzania and Kenya. It also affected Syria, Yemen and Nigeria. At the time, a large proportion of each of these countries was Muslim.

The following is a list of the countries in the world which have more than 50% Muslims as of 2008:
Sierra Leone, Guinea, Gambia, Senegal, Mauritania, Mali, Niger, Western Sahara, Morocco, Algeria, Tunisia, Libya, Chad, Egypt, Sudan, Turkey, Syria, Lebanon, Iraq, Jordan, Kuwait, Saudi Arabia, Yemen, Djibouti, Somalia, Oman, United Arab Emirates, Qatar, Bahrain, Iran, Pakistan, Afghanistan, Turkmenistan, Uzbekistan, Kazakhstan, Kyrgyzstan, Tajikistan, Malaysia, Indonesia, Brunei, Singapore.

Of all these countries, only Sierra Leone, Guinea, Gambia, Brunei, Malaysia, Indonesia and Singapore do not fall within the region of low annual rainfall indicated on the map. Yet we have already seen that God in recent years has judged Indonesia and Gambia severely. What then of Sierra Leone, Guinea, Malaysia, Philippines and Brunei? Sierra Leone has suffered terribly from war and poverty. Guinea has also not been without afflictions with poverty and disease looming large. Between 1975 and 2000 37,000 have died in the Philippines as a result of 250 natural disasters. Similarly, Malaysia has suffered dreadfully from flooding. Only Brunei has seemed to escape the judgment of God. The country is rich with large oil reserves and high rainfall. Yet at the same time she has excluded missionaries from the country and it is illegal for Christians to give the gospel to Muslims. It would seem to me that it is only the mercy of God that has caused her to escape so far.

United States of America

In the next chapter we will look further at God's judgment of America, but at this stage I will make mention of just four occasions when God judged America for her disobedience.

In the years leading up to 1857, 'the city and the country had been absorbed in the pursuit of pleasure and gain. Men were making haste to be rich, and to enjoy their riches. Recklessness of expenditure, extravagance in living, display in furniture, equipage, and dress, had attained a height unexampled in the previous social history of [the] country...'[26] Then suddenly the New York branch of the Ohio Life Insurance and Trust Company closed. This led to a run on the banks in the east of America, spreading as far as Omaha. What compounded the panic was the sinking of *SS Central America.* At the time she was sailing from San Francisco to New York with a cargo which included fifteen tons of gold. This was valued at $20 an ounce. At this time financial institutions traded in gold rather than paper money and this gold was to provide a reserve for the banks in the east. The ramifications were obviously huge. But why did the ship sink? The ship sailed right into a severe hurricane. The Lord had judged the nation by bringing down her financial institutions, partly by causing chaos to grip the country and partly by sending a severe storm. The wonderful part of it all, though, was the fact that in 1858 New York found herself in the grip of a revival. The connection has been noted by many including Samuel Prime, who wrote: 'The autumn of 1857 was signalized by a sudden and fearful convulsion in the commercial world.

That calamity was so speedily followed by the reports of revival of religion and remarkable displays of divine grace, that it has been a widely received opinion, that the two events stand related to one another, as cause and effect. In the day of adversity, men consider.'[27]

Another example of God judging America came in response to her treatment of the land. When the law was given by God, a fundamental aspect was the keeping of the sabbath, a day of rest from all labour. Interestingly, this sabbath was extended to the land. Every seven years the land was to lie fallow that it might rest and its resources replenished. God said that if the people failed to do this he would force a sabbath upon the land:

> Then shall the land enjoy her sabbaths, as long as it lieth desolate, and ye be in your enemies' land; even then shall the land rest, and enjoy her sabbaths. As long as it lieth desolate it shall rest; because it did not rest in your sabbaths, when ye dwelt upon it (Leviticus 26:34–35).

In the 1930s settlers moved to the Great Plains and began intensively farming the prairieland. Without the grass the wind swept away the soil.

> Several years of dry weather added to the problem for the weary farmers. There was a popular belief that 'rain would follow the plow,' but rain did not come. The dust was like rolling black smoke and sometimes suffocated cattle in its path. It covered fences and almost buried farm houses. In places large depressions over one hundred feet deep formed in farm fields, called dust bowls. Some of these eroded areas have never recovered, even after sixty years.[28]

As a side note, the Lord has ensured that the land of Britain also has received its rest. In recent times farmers have been able to receive subsidies from the European Union to leave the land fallow as sites of natural interest. Farmers across the country have been taking advantage of these benefits and so the land is once more receiving its sabbath. However, this has meant that the earth is no longer fruitful and the nation has become increasingly dependent upon other nations for its produce.

Thirdly, on October 17th 1989 San Francisco was struck by one of the largest earthquakes to hit America that century. It came to be known as the Loma Prieta earthquake. Ultimately registering 7.1 on the Richter scale it had a devastating effect on the state. What is most significant in the light of this book is that two days previously San Francisco was the site of a pro-abortion rally which attracted 50,000 people. The rally had taken place outside City Hall. When the earthquake struck City Hall suffered serious damage. The very place where Americans called for the continuation of the murder of unborn children, God poured out his wrath. Yet God was still merciful in that only 67 people died.

Finally, on January 17th 1994 an earthquake registering 6.7 hit Los Angeles. The epicentre was Northridge which is the centre of the pornography industry in America.

These four events each demonstrate the direct link between natural disasters and the judgment of God.

Japan

State Shintoism incorporates the belief that the emperor is divine, the emperor being 'elevated to the status of "sacred and inviolable" head of state'.[29] This cult was re-established in Japan in 1868 and came to the fore in the 1920s and 1930s. The assertion that the emperor was descended from the gods led to the belief in the superiority of the Japanese race, which in turn led to Japanese expansionist foreign policy during the 1930s. Moreover, State Shintoism decreed that every person was to give himself to the state, which resulted in the introduction of kamikaze pilots. In the light of this replacement of the living God with a man, is it any wonder that Japan came under severe judgment from God? Three of the most deadly tsunamis of the twentieth century struck Japan when State Shintoism was at its height. These took place in 1923, 1933 and 1944 and in total killed over 11,000 people.[30] What is more, the Tsunami of 1923 was triggered by an earthquake that killed between 100,000 and 142,000.

In 1995 there was another earthquake which struck Kobe and Osaka. 5,500 died in total. 'Many of the Shinto shrines and Buddhist temples were destroyed and in some areas the church was virtually the only building left standing. The churches were able to provide a place of sanctuary for many people as well as running soup kitchens, some feeding up to 500 people a day.'[31] Japan was also affected by a major financial crisis in the 1990s. God used both to judge the nation for its complacency and denial of God.

China
It might be argued that China has had more than its fair share of natural disasters. Five of the ten deadliest natural disasters in history have occurred in China, including the two worst. By death-toll, four of the ten worst earthquakes have occurred in China, the four worst typhoons, six of the ten worst floods, including the five worst floods, five of the ten worst famines including the two worst. Many natural explanations might be given for why China has suffered exponentially more than any other country in the

world, the two most obvious being her high population and geographical location. However, as we have already seen, God is sovereign and nothing happens outside of his control.

This leaves us with the question, why has China suffered so greatly? In terms of God's dealings with this nation it would seem as though her history can be divided into two. Prior to 1949 it was a place of extreme idolatry. In 1949 the Communist Party took power and China was declared an atheistic state. Is it any wonder then that the God who is a jealous God, should judge a nation that has throughout her history vehemently rejected him?

God and the continents

In spite of all that has been said, the reader may still be left pondering why it is that the great land masses of Africa and Asia suffer exponentially more than all other continents. It takes a man born and brought up in India to answer this question. K. P. Yohannan, President and founder of Gospel for Asia, writes:

> Few Westerners, when they see news reports of the poverty, suffering and violence in Asia, take time to stop and ask why the East is bound into an endless cycle of suffering while Western nations are so blessed.
>
> Secular humanists are quick to reel out many historic and pseudoscientific reasons for the disparity, because they are unwilling to face the truth. But the real reason is simple: The Judeo-Christian heritage of Europe has brought the favour of God, while false religions have brought the curse of Babylon on other nations.
>
> Mature Christians realize the Bible teaches there are

only two religions in this world. There is the worship of the one true God, and there is a false system invented in ancient Persia. From there, Persian armies and priests spread their faith to India, where it took root. Its missionaries in turn spread it throughout the rest of Asia. Animism and all other Asian religions have a common heritage in this one religious system.[32]

I would suggest that much of what K. P. Yohannan writes regarding Asia could be applied to Africa. It is certainly true that many of the people living on this vast continent are bound by witchcraft and animism. It is also true that their foundations are not built on Judeo-Christian principles.

The Bible says that 'we wrestle not against flesh and blood, but against principalities, against powers, against the rulers of the darkness of this world, against spiritual wickedness in high places' (Ephesians 6:12). Everything we see around us must be viewed from the perspective of the spiritual battle that we are involved in. To look at the poverty and suffering in huge parts of the world without any recourse to the spiritual cause is to reduce the world to the material. We look at North America, Australasia and Europe and see the contrast with Asia in particular, but also vast tracts of Africa. However, there is a reason and it is that Europe, North America and Australasia are rooted in the Judeo-Christian faith. Are these places Christian? Certainly not, but their institutions, government and laws are built upon biblical truth. However, each of these continents currently stands in a perilous position. Each of these continents has over recent decades broken up those foundations. The Christian faith has become something to be mocked and ridiculed. We are now witnessing the shift from blessing to curse for much of the West. Many might suggest that this has been going on for some time.

When a nation throws off all moral restraint and travels the path of wickedness, history testifies to God's judgment and wrath being poured forth. God is not silent and no matter how the world may attempt to shut him out of their lives, God still speaks. He speaks in the earthquake, the flood and the hurricane.

8

God Rescues the Righteous

One obvious question that arises when wrestling with the issue of God's judgment and the nations is what happens to the believer. If a nation is judged the question comes, is the Christian who lives there judged too?

In many ways this is not a straightforward question to answer. Certainly the Bible promises us that Christ is our shelter in the storm and the flood and that in the midst of drought he will provide for his people:

> For this shall every one that is godly pray unto thee in a time when thou mayest be found: surely in the floods of great waters they shall not come nigh unto him. Thou art my hiding place; thou shalt preserve me from trouble; thou shalt compass me about with songs of deliverance (Psalm 32:6–7. See also Isaiah 58:11).

Yet it would not be difficult to find instances in history when those who have been trusting in Christ have died as a result of a storm, flood or drought. This leaves us with the dilemma, do we continue to hold firm to the promises

of the Bible, or do we jettison the word of God in the face
of experience?

Certainly God is the only true foundation which we
have. Therefore, we must ask questions of our experience
in the light of what the word of God says. However, we
must begin by establishing the fact that God does deliver
the righteous in the midst of judgment:

> They shall not hunger nor thirst; neither shall the heat
> nor sun smite them: for he that hath mercy on them
> shall lead them, even by the springs of water shall he
> guide them (Isaiah 49:10).
>
> For he shall be as a tree planted by the waters, and
> that spreadeth out her roots by the river, and shall not
> see when heat cometh, but her leaf shall be green; and
> shall not be careful in the year of drought, neither shall
> cease from yielding fruit (Jeremiah 17:8).

God does provide shelter and protection for his people. He
has made that promise to us. Numerous events recorded in
the Bible bear testimony to this fact.

God saves Noah and his family

In the light of the fact that God judged the whole earth
with the Flood, it is significant that God saved just eight
people as a result of Noah's righteousness. In the midst of
judgment God delivered his people:

> Noah found grace in the eyes of the Lord. ...Noah was
> a just man and perfect in his generations, and Noah
> walked with God. (Genesis 6:8–9).

It is noteworthy that it is only Noah who is mentioned as
being righteous, yet his family is saved. There is certainly

a principle that just as God delivers the righteous, so on occasions he delivers from judgment those who are directly associated with the righteous:

> And the LORD said unto Noah, Come thou and all thy house into the ark; for thee have I seen righteous before me in this generation (Genesis 7:1).

The children of Israel in the wilderness

When the children of Israel were delivered by the hand of the Lord out of Egypt, they were taken by way of the desert, and during the forty years of wandering God led and protected them. The word of God bears testimony to this:

> ...The LORD thy God, which brought thee forth out of the land of Egypt, ...who led thee through that great and terrible wilderness, wherein were fiery serpents, and scorpions, and drought, where there was no water; who brought thee forth water out of the rock of flint; who fed thee in the wilderness with manna... (Deuteronomy 8:14–16).

Even though the wilderness did not provide any water, and was a place where no one dwelt, the Lord provided protection for his people. He provided water, manna and quails to sustain them. Even though they had to endure that place the Lord provided for their needs. In the midst of the drought God was their shelter and sustenance.

Elijah, the widow and her son

During Elijah's lifetime there was a time when there was neither rain nor dew in the land of Israel. We later learn that the reason for such a calamity was because Ahab and his father's house had 'forsaken the commandments of the LORD, and... followed Baalim' (1 Kings 18:18). In the midst of this drought God provided both for Elijah and a widow and her son.

The Lord first commanded Elijah to go to the brook Cherith. The word of God tells us that 'the ravens brought him bread and flesh in the morning, and bread and flesh in the evening; and he drank of the brook' (I Kings 17:6). In due course the brook dried up and the Lord once more spoke to him, commanding him to go to Zarephath. There he met a widow who was gathering sticks to prepare a final meal for her and her son. Yet Elijah tells her to make him a cake. She does as Elijah commands her, responding in faith to the word of the Lord that Elijah brought to her:

> For thus saith the LORD God of Israel, The barrel of meal shall not waste, neither shall the cruse of oil fail, until the day that the LORD sendeth rain upon the earth (I Kings 17:14).

The Lord blessed that woman and provided for her because she blessed Elijah, one of God's prophets, and because she trusted the Lord. Throughout the Bible we find those who bless God's people and trust in the Lord are blessed and delivered. Though God had commanded a drought to be upon the land he still protected his own. Elijah, the widow and her son bear testimony to the Lord's provision and protection in the midst of judgment.

This still leaves us with the question that we posed at the beginning, why do some Christians suffer as a result of storms, floods and drought when God has promised to protect and deliver his people? Psalm 32 provides the answer:

> For this shall every one that is godly pray unto thee in a time when thou mayest be found: surely in the floods of great waters they shall not come nigh unto him. Thou art my hiding place; thou shalt preserve me from trouble; thou shalt compass me about with songs of deliverance. (Psalm 32:6–7).

The Christian is able to know protection in the midst of the flood and drought by trusting and obeying the Lord. It is through godliness (holiness) and being yielded to the Lord through prayer that the individual comes under the shelter of the Lord.

It is possible to be born again but not completely trust him and live in full obedience to him. When this is the case we cannot expect to know his full hand of protection upon our lives. The way to know God's deliverance is to trust and obey. Failure to do so completely does not mean that we cease from being saved eternally, but it does mean that we come out from being under the shelter of his wings.

God's deliverance of his people is certainly not confined to Scripture. Christians all over the world, and in various situations, are able to bear testimony to God's grace in delivering them in the midst of storms and floods. However, I just want to make mention of two particular acts of God's grace in recent times.

Boxing Day Tsunami

The Indian Ocean Tsunami, which took placing on 26th December 2004, became known as the Boxing Day Tsunami. However, the events of the preceding days show how God is sovereign over all things and all people. In the midst of persecution and in a strict Muslim country, the Christians living in the city had requested to celebrate the birth of their Saviour. They were refused initially, but in due course they were given permission to celebrate and worship the Lord as long as they did so outside the city. The Christians departed for the hills. Over the Christmas period they remained there and when the Tsunami came they were high above the waves below. God in his mercy and sovereignty had rescued his people from the storm and the waves. A wonderful deliverance in the midst of judgment had taken place.

Another instance of God's deliverance in the midst of the Tsunami took place at an orphanage. In Navalady, Sri Lanka, a missionary-run orphanage was situated by a lagoon, and as such was directly in the path of the wave. As they saw the wave heading straight for the orphanage, they hurriedly gathered everyone together and got them aboard the orphanage's motor boat. Now normally the motor was removed each evening, and had that been the case it would have delayed them so much that they would not have been able to escape before the tsunami hit. It was only because someone had failed to remove the motor the previous evening that they were able to get away so quickly. Moreover, whereas it always took several attempts to get the boat started, on this occasion it started immediately. Consequently, everyone in the orphanage was saved.[33]

What a wonderful example of God's deliverance. Those that seek and trust the Lord have the promise that they will be delivered. This should lead the believer to have his eyes always fixed on Jesus. He is the shelter in the storm. When a nation experiences the wrath and judgment of God, those that walk righteously before the Lord will be preserved.

9

God Blesses the Nations

While we have established the fact that God does indeed use the elements to bring judgment upon a nation, a city or an individual, we must remember that God is a merciful God. The Bible makes it clear that God shows favour to those nations that humble themselves before him, and the Bible spells out clearly that one of the ways the Lord's goodness is manifest is by good weather. Two passages stand out by way of setting out this principle. The first is found in Deuteronomy 28, which deals with the blessings and curses that will fall upon a people that either obeys or disobeys God.

> ...all these blessings shall come on thee, and overtake thee, if thou shalt hearken unto the voice of the LORD thy God. Blessed shalt thou be in the city, and blessed shalt thou be in the field. ...The LORD shall command the blessing upon thee in thy storehouses, and in all that thou settest thine hand unto; and he shall bless thee in the land which the LORD thy God giveth thee. ...And the LORD shall make thee plenteous in goods ... in the fruit of thy ground. ...The LORD shall open unto

thee his good treasure, the heaven to give the rain unto thy land in his season, and to bless all the work of thine hand (Deuteronomy 28:2–3, 8, 11–12).

When God promises to bless the storehouse and the work of their hands, he is in effect saying, 'I will command the elements, over which you have no control, to do the work of bringing forth much fruit.' Even if we work hard in the field, if there is no rain the crops will wither and die. Without the sun the crops will not ripen. However, when God speaks, commanding a blessing, the land produces its fruit and the storehouse is filled. This blessing is in the hand of God to give as he pleases, and he has promised to bestow it upon those who are obedient to him and walk in his ways.

The second passage that clearly proves the relationship between submission to God and the blessing of good weather, is found in I Kings. Quoted below is part of Solomon's prayer of dedication of the temple to God:

When heaven is shut up, and there is no rain, because they have sinned against thee; if they pray toward this place, and confess thy name, and turn from their sin, when thou afflictest them: then hear thou in heaven, and forgive the sin of thy people Israel... and give rain upon thy land (I Kings 8:35–36; c.f. II Chronicles 6:26–27).

Solomon is concerned with what should happen if the people turn away from the Lord and suffer judgment. He asks that the Lord will forgive the people and once more give them rain if they repent. The Lord then appears to him and assures him that he has heard his prayer and supplication:

> And the LORD appeared to Solomon by night, and said unto him, I have heard thy prayer, and have chosen this place to myself for an house of sacrifice. If I shut up heaven that there be no rain, or if I command the locusts to devour the land, or if I send pestilence among my people; if my people, which are called by my name, shall humble themselves, and pray, and seek my face, and turn from their wicked ways, then will I hear from heaven, and will forgive their sin, and will heal their land (II Chronicles 7:12–14).

It is by turning from sin and returning to the Lord that a nation will once more know God's blessing. Sin is the cause of the judgment of God coming upon a nation and repentance is the means by which a nation will know the blessing of God. Let us look at some examples of how God used particular types of weather to bless.

Rain

It is true that rain may be used by the Lord in judgment. Indeed, we have seen this already, the clearest example being the Flood. Yet rain is essential for life, and God promises to send forth the rain to a nation which obeys him. It is God who sends the rain and when a nation receives the rain at the right time then it is a demonstration of God's mercy. Rain that falls when it is not the right season is no blessing at all; in fact it is a curse. Consider a farmer who has worked all year and is now ready to bring in the harvest. Just as he is about to do so the rains fall day after day. The crops will be ruined. Rain is not a blessing then.

Yet a nation that is blessed will know the provision of the rain at the right time, *in his season*:

> If ye walk in my statutes, and keep my commandments, and do them; then I will give you rain in due season, and the land shall yield her increase, and the trees of the field shall yield their fruit. And your threshing shall reach unto the vintage, and the vintage shall reach unto the sowing time: and ye shall eat your bread to the full, and dwell in your land safely. ...And ye shall eat old store, and bring forth the old because of the new (Leviticus 26:3–5, 10, c.f. Deuteronomy 11:13–14).

Throughout the Bible we witness God blessing people with rain.

One particular example of God responding to the repentance of the people is found in I Kings. Chapter eighteen records how Elijah defeated the prophets of Baal and showed that the Lord was the true God when he called on him to send fire down on the sacrifice that he had prepared. On seeing the altar and the sacrifice burnt up the people responded by falling on their faces, saying; 'The Lord, he is the God; the Lord, he is the God' (I Kings 18:39). Soon after, the heaven was black with clouds and wind, and there was a great rain (I Kings 18:45). There had been a great drought in the land and now as the people repented from following Baal, God spoke from heaven by commanding the clouds to pour forth rain upon the land.

God makes a similar promise in response to repentance in Joel:

> Therefore also now, saith the Lord, turn ye even to me with all your heart, and with fasting, and with

weeping, and with mourning: and rend your heart, and not your garments, and turn unto the LORD your God... The LORD will answer and say unto his people, Behold, I will send you corn, and wine, and oil, and ye shall be satisfied therewith: and I will no more make you a reproach among the heathen... The LORD will do great things... The pastures of the wilderness do spring, for the tree beareth her fruit, the fig tree and the vine do yield their strength. Be glad then, ye children of Zion, and rejoice in the LORD your God: for he hath given you the former rain moderately, and he will cause to come down for you the rain, the former rain, and the latter rain in the first month (Joel 2:12–13, 19, 21–23).

The clear implication is that because of the sin of the nation the heavens had been closed and there was a famine upon the land. The former rain refers to the rain which would descend at the time of sowing, while the latter rain came immediately before the harvest. Both were necessary for a good harvest. Though there had been a drought, if the people repented, God promised to make the land fruitful by providing the former and latter rain.

Sun

While the heat of the sun may bring great affliction, we also know that without it there would be no seedtime, harvest, or summer. God has set the sun in the heavens and determined its courses for our benefit. Without the sun the earth would not yield its fruit:

And this is the blessing, wherewith Moses the man of God blessed the children of Israel before his death. ...And of Joseph he said, Blessed of the LORD be his land, for the precious things of heaven, for the dew, and for the deep that coucheth beneath, and for the precious fruits brought forth by the sun... (Deuteronomy 33:1, 13–14a).

Snow

We might easily associate rain and the sun with God's blessing but I wonder if we would say the same of snow. It is certainly true that snow can have harmful effects. When it is heaped upon the land it brings destruction. However, Donald De Young has pointed to a number of benefits of snow, thus showing the goodness of God. First, 'snow provides a slow, measured supply of water to underground water reservoirs.'[34] This is important since if the same water came down in the form of rain much of it would drain away and would not be stored.

> The rain cometh down, and the snow from heaven, and returneth not thither, but watereth the earth, and maketh it bring forth and bud, that it may give seed to the sower, and bread to the eater... (Isaiah 55:10).

Second, rather surprisingly, snow actually acts as an insulator for the earth below. We might associate snow with the cold, but a blanket of snow stops the earth freezing and protects animals which are able to bury beneath the snow during the winter months. Third, it purifies the air by collecting particles and removing them from the atmosphere. As De Young observes, 'the whiteness of snowflakes is a suitable metaphor for God's cleansing of our sin.'[35]

Lightning

In a previous chapter we saw how God uses thunder and lightning to judge the nations. Lightning, it is true, demonstrates God's authority and power to a people who have rejected him as Lord. However, even in the midst of judgment we find mercy. As humans we need a daily supply of nitrogen. We might think that this wouldn't be a problem since the air is mainly made up of nitrogen. However, our bodies are unable to absorb nitrogen without its being transformed into a nitrate, NO_3. Certain plants are able to do this themselves. We are then able to benefit by eating those vegetables or by eating animals which have eaten them. However, lightning causes oxygen and nitrogen to join together in the form of oxides of nitrogen. Most of them are soluble in water. Plants are then able to absorb nitrogen in this form. By eating these plants we are able to get the nitrogen we need. Therefore, when we see lightning flashes we should be mindful of the authority and power, but also of the goodness of the One who

directeth... his lightning unto the ends of the earth (Job 37:3).

Clouds

The Bible makes clear that even the clouds are governed by God. Clouds not only help to control the earth's temperature, but are God's means of blessing the earth with rain:

For he maketh small the drops of water: they pour down rain according to the vapour thereof: which the clouds do drop and distil upon man abundantly (Job 36:27–28).

God does indeed bless the nations, and the word of God makes it clear that when a nation walks in obedience before him they will know his blessing by the provision of rain, sunshine and even snow. A nation that has turned from the

Lord but subsequently repents will, though it has known calamity, subsequently know the blessing of the Lord.

10

The Weather, God's Blessing and Modern History

As we have seen, God blesses those who walk humbly before him. In particular, God said that if a people who have turned away from him once more humble themselves before him, he will heal their land. History bears witness to God's provision of rain and sunshine to those who have repented and trusted in him. Not only that, God uses the weather to show his mercy to those who seek his face.

Dunkirk

Numerous times during the Second World War Britain experienced God's wonderful mercy, protection and deliverance. Three events stand out for our attention. The first is the famous Dunkirk rescue when a flotilla of ships, boats and sailing vessels left these shores to rescue the British troops stranded on the coast of France. The German army had advanced so far that without a daring rescue these men had no hope. It was this that caused the Government to call on every person who owned a vessel fit to cross the English Channel to ready himself to sail. On that night, when all manner of boats set forth to make that treacherous voyage, the Channel was said to be as still as a millpond. The conditions were perfect for sailing. What is more, a mist descended upon the sea. God covered those vessels from the sight of the enemy. God had spoken to the elements, they obeyed, and the men were saved. On that night God showed his mighty hand of deliverance.

Perhaps just as extraordinary, and something that many at the time acknowledged to be the work of God, was the storm that raged over Dunkirk prior to the landings. David Gardner writes the following:

> A storm of unprecedented fury broke over Flanders on Tuesday, 28 May, grounding the German Luftwaffe squadrons and enabling the British army formations, now eight to twelve miles from Dunkirk, to move up on foot to the coast in the darkness of the storm and the violence of the rain, with scarcely any interruption from aircraft, which were unable to operate in such turbulent conditions. ...Despite the storm in Flanders, a great calm – such as has rarely been experienced – settled over the English Channel... Yet still, to a very large extent, the German air squadrons were unable to intervene. Certainly not in force, nor in the way Hitler had anticipated, for so many of these squadrons still remained grounded. So much so that General Halder, Chief of the German General Staff, three days after the High Command had so proudly boasted that the British Army was about to be annihilated, was obliged to record in his diary on 30 May that 'Bad weather has grounded the Luftwaffe, and now we must stand by and watch countless thousands of the enemy getting away to England right under our noses.'[36]

Lest any one should say the prayers of a nation are not effective, let us remember that King George VI called for Sunday 26th May to be a National Day of Prayer. Churches across the land were packed with people calling on the Lord for deliverance. Dunkirk is proof that God answers the humble cries of a nation in distress.

Normandy Landings

As the war was nearing its end, once more the people of Britain found themselves dependent upon the Lord's mercy for victory. The decision had been made to launch an attack combining the army, navy and air-force of both Britain and America. The plan was that in a single, co-ordinated effort the deliverance of France would be accomplished. However, success was dependent upon good weather and clear skies. Day after day preceding the attack, the wind and waves raged making it seem as though the plan would have to be put back. However, finally, meteorologists observed that a twenty-four hour period would occur when the storm would dissipate and the clouds would be broken. This is indeed what happened. Had it occurred any later, the whole operation would have had to have been called off. On that day God provided the conditions for the boats to sail, for the false harbours to be set up on the beaches of Normandy, and for the planes to attack. God had once more acted.

Yet we must remember that God was also controlling the preceding storm. The storm had caused the German leaders to discount any invasion at this time. Indeed, when the forces stepped ashore they found the enemy totally unprepared for battle. God had caused the storm and subsequently had caused the winds to be still. So France was delivered and Germany edged nearer to final surrender.

Once more the prayers of a nation had been answered,

for the day before D-Day, King George VI made this broadcast:

> Four years ago our nation and empire stood alone against an overwhelming enemy, with our backs to the wall. Tested as never before in our history, in God's providence we survived that test.
>
> The spirit of the people, resolute, dedicated, burned like a bright flame, lit surely from those unseen fires which nothing can quench.
>
> Now once more a supreme test has to be faced.
>
> This time the challenge is not to fight to survive but to fight to win the final victory for the good cause....
>
> That we may be worthily matched with this new summons of destiny, I desire solemnly to call my people to prayer and to dedication.
>
> We are not unmindful of our shortcomings, past and present.
>
> We shall ask not that God may do our will, but that we may be enabled to do the will of God.
>
> And we dare to believe that God has used our nation and empire as an instrument for fulfilling his high purpose. Surely not one of us is too busy to play our part in a nation-wide, perchance a world-wide, vigil of prayer as the great crusade sets forth.[37]

God provides a bumper harvest

The final intervention of God during the war that demands mentioning is the bumper harvest of 1942. God, in Britain's hour of need, provided her with a wonderful blessing that even the government acknowledged. Facing food shortages as a result of the War, God gave the nation what she needed. O that our leaders would follow the example of those who led this country during the Second World War, and give praise to God for his bountiful supply. Tragically, seldom do we hear even Christians giving God glory for his marvellous provision.

Other testimonies to God's blessing

In an earlier chapter we pointed to the fact that the decisions taken by the king or leader of a nation have serious ramifications for the land over which he rules. Though a king who rules in unrighteousness will see the nation suffer God's judgment, a king who rules in submission to God will see the land blessed. A wonderful example of the latter occurred in Lesotho in 1999. Even the secular media recognised God's answer to the prayers of a king and of a nation. The BBC website reported at the time that King Letsie of Lesotho called the nation to pray for rain because the land was experiencing a severe drought. As the people returned home from church they were soaked by a downpour. [38]

Miracle in Kenya

Orus in northern Kenya had suffered two years of drought. The area had therefore certainly known the judgment of God. However, the following testimony to God's mercy demonstrates what we have already seen, namely, that repentance from sin and turning to God is the way in which God's judgment on a nation is brought to an end.

A missionary had come to the area, telling of the salvation to be found in Jesus Christ. One day, an old diviner asked if the missionary's God could send the rain. He, along with other diviners, had made sacrifices to their gods but no rain had come. The following is part of a report of what happened, posted on the Global Connections website:

> The old man scornfully said, "God has thrown us away. He hasn't heard any of our prayers!" Then he said, "If your God is so great see if he will send rain!"
>
> The people anxiously gathered around. The missionary told them, "First we must repent of all our sins. He explained to them that they had sinned by stealing cattle from the next door tribe and even killed others in the raiding. Then I told them we had to pray in Jesus' name alone." The people all agreed except the old man.
>
> [The missionary] prayed in Swahili and each sentence was translated into Pokot. Like Elijah they thought they would see a cloud in the sky. But there was none. The next day as they left for another town about 25 miles away to buy supplies, they looked back and saw a huge dark cloud just over the Orus area where they had prayed.
>
> They were greeted with the news [on their return] that it had rained every day since they left and only at Orus!
>
> During the next Sunday service, the old diviner stood before the people and said, "Truly it is Jesus who has power with God."[39]

South Africa

In 1977 South Africa suffered a drought that was having severe consequences. In the light of this the president called for a National Day of Repentance. Two days later the rains came. It should be noted that neither F W de Klerk, Nelson Mandela nor Thabo Mbeki have called the nation to repent, inspite of the fact that South Africa has suffered drought many times during their leadership.

China

A final example of God's merciful provision of rain in response to the prayers of God's people occurred in China in 1999:

> "It had not rained in China's northern provinces for 5 years," reports the Singapore arm of the evangelical missions agency OMF following the return of a Chinese pastor, some American visitors and several government officials from a tour of villages hit by the drought. The situation seemed hopeless. Local officials reported that high-ranking members of the government had visited the area the previous year, but were unable to help significantly because of the lack of water. Suddenly, one of the officials turned to the visitors, asking "Can your God make it rain in the next 20 days?" Without batting an eyelid, the Chinese pastor answered "Yes, of course he can." "So pray that it happens," the official told him. "If it rains in the next 20 days, we will know that it was your God who did it." 12 days later, it rained significantly in the northern provinces. "Now we believe that your God really answers prayer," said the officials.[40]

The healing of Fiji

The Bible makes it plain that when a nation's leaders along with the people humble themselves before God, he will heal their land. Fiji is a nation that in recent years has been able to bear testimony to this. The following is taken from *Prophecy Today*:

> The President, Prime Minister and many top government officials have become deeply committed Christians and have led the way in calling the Church to repentance. Church leaders report that even members of the military who led the coup three years ago – now in prison – have turned to Christ for forgiveness. ...A phenomenon of the Fijian revival is God's miraculous regeneration of nature. Coral reefs are being restored following decades of disintegration, shoals of fish are returning to the islands' waters and rivers, and crabs are walking on the beaches for the first time in years. Fruit is again growing on the trees and the vines are flourishing.
>
> Forty years earlier an intense tribal war had filled the valley with death, desperation and fear. At the height of the conflict, a stream that ran through the centre of the village suddenly clouded and became bitter. Drinking from the stream could lead to madness, blindness and other terrible problems. Government tests of the water found arsenic, tar and other poisonous substances. ...Recently, several village women discovered that the water had suddenly become crystal clear. ...It had become drinkable again!'[41]

God and his Land

In the Book of Job we are told that rain is either for correction, mercy, or *for his land*:

> ...by watering he wearieth the thick cloud: he scattereth his bright cloud: And it is turned round about by his

counsels: that they may do whatsoever he commandeth
them upon the face of the world in the earth. He causeth
it to come, whether for correction, or for his land, or for
mercy (Job 37:11-13).

We have already seen how God controls the elements for
his purposes in bringing correction and mercy. Now we
find that God uses the weather *for his land*. What does this
mean and what are the consequences for us?

First we must understand what land is being referred to
here. It refers to the whole earth, including the uninhabited
places, because a little further on in the Book of Job, it
says:

To cause it to rain on the earth, where no man is; on
the wilderness, wherein there is no man; to satisfy the
desolate and waste ground; and to cause the bud of the
tender herb to spring forth... (Job 38:26).

The provision of rain for 'his land' is to be seen in the context
of God's provision of life to the earth. It is not only the
wilderness that knows God's care, but also the mountains:

Sing unto the LORD with thanksgiving; sing praise
upon the harp unto our God: who covereth the heaven
with clouds, who prepareth rain for the earth, who
maketh grass to grow upon the mountains. He giveth
to the beast his food, and to the young ravens which
cry (Psalm 147:7–9).

God's provision of rain, and by implication sun etc., are
not just manifestations of his mercy, justice and judgment,
but also demonstrations of his care for the earth that he

has created. He watches over the whole earth and he is the one whom the whole earth is dependent upon for life and blessing. The grass grows, the wild animals are fed and the desolate places bring forth their fruit, because of the mighty hand of God who provides all things bounteously.

Just as creation and the nations bear witness to God's power, so the rain and the seasons are a testimony to God's goodness. Mankind is the recipient of God's kindness:

> ...ye should turn from these vanities unto the living God, which made heaven, and earth, and the sea, and all things that are therein: who in times past suffered all nations to walk in their own ways. Nevertheless he left not himself without witness, in that he did good, and gave us rain from heaven, and fruitful seasons, filling our hearts with food and gladness (Acts 14:15–17).

11

The Weather and God's Providence

God's use of the weather goes beyond blessing and judgment. He also commands the weather to bring about his purposes, both in the lives of individuals and nations. As we saw in an earlier chapter, when Paul was sailing to Rome under arrest, a storm arose which led to his arrival on the island of Milita. As we observed then, it was the providence of God that ensured that Paul ended up being on that particular island. History bears further testimony to the fact that God uses the weather to bring about his sovereign plans.

A particular example of this occurred in 1948 in America. The election in that year was between Dewey and Truman, and everything right up to the day of the election suggested that Dewey would win. Truman, who was a Democrat, had suffered in the run up to the election as a result of some from his own party leaving to form their own. On the day of the election the polls made it clear that Dewey was going to win. However, the weather had something else to say about that, or rather God did.

In America, elections are fought on a state by state basis, and whoever wins the most votes in a state gains all the electoral votes for that particular state. Laura Lee, on the effect the weather had on the election result, observed that on the day of the election rain spread across Illinois. It has been argued that at the time the Democrats benefited from the rain because Republican voters who lived in rural areas had greater difficulty getting to the polling stations than the urban voters who tended to be Democrats. Furthermore, the storm mostly affected the rural district. This played into the hands of Democrats in Illinois. A second storm led to rain in California. Extraordinarily, the Republican north received rain, while the Democrat south had sun. Fewer than thirty thousand votes could have changed the election result. The end result was that Truman won by 303 to 189 electoral votes.[42]

Whether Britain's return to Protestantism at the end of the seventeenth century was due to any repentance on the people's part, it is hard to say. However, once more, the weather played a key role. God spoke, the wind blew, and William and Mary took their predestined places upon the throne of England.

In 1687 James II, a Catholic, was on the throne. At this stage he was without child and if he failed to have a son, on his death the throne would pass to his sister Mary Stuart who was the wife of William of Orange. However, in 1688 James II did have a son thus causing consternation amongst the Protestants in England at the time. In the mean-time William and Mary were attempting to sail to England from Holland with the purpose of taking the throne. However, when they tried the winds were against them and they were unable to set sail. When they did finally depart for England a storm arose causing the fleet to have to retreat to port. News reached England that the fleet had suffered severe loss. Eventually however, William and Mary set sail again and on arrival at the mouth of the English Channel the wind blew enabling them to sail right up the Channel. When they set foot on English soil they found no armies to meet them for James II had presumed that now he would not be attacked.

The wind that had prevented William and Mary from sailing initially led to James II being unprepared. Following this, God, in his perfect timing, caused the wind to enable them to sail up the English Channel. Finally, he caused a south-westerly wind to blow to prevent James II's fleet from gaining access to the Channel. God was in control, and by way of the wind he ensured that a Protestant king would once more be upon the throne of England.

God also uses the weather to change the destiny of an individual. We can see this act of grace in the life of John Newton. On one voyage, as a slave trader, he found himself in a dreadful storm. Amidst the great storm he had begun to climb up a ladder to get to the deck. Immediately, however, he was sent down to fetch a knife. As he reached the bottom a gigantic wave hit the ladder.[43] As a result of his errand his life was spared. It was while the storm still raged that Newton cried out to God for mercy, God responded and the result was a soul saved. God sent the storm to bring Newton to his knees, but in bringing him to his knees, the Lord subsequently raised him up to fulfil his purposes in ending the slave trade.

God is sovereign. Nothing and no-one can thwart his purposes. He has a myriad ways of bringing about his will and one of these is the weather. He commands the wind and the rain and they obey him. He uses each in turn to alter circumstances and ensure that his plans are brought about.

12

God and Israel

In recent years, the subject of Israel has caused much debate within Christian circles. The controversy has largely centred round two connected issues. The first is whether God has finished with Israel, and that consequently, she is no longer under his particular blessing. The second is whether the Church has replaced Israel, and consequently the blessing that Israel once knew has been passed to the Church.

At this point you are probably thinking, *What does Israel have to do with the weather we experience from day to day?* As I hope to show, in fact our weather is intrinsically tied up with Israel, perhaps not on a daily basis, but certainly periodically.

In dealing with the connection between the weather and the nation of Israel we must first understand the nature of the covenant God originally made with Israel. God's covenant with Israel can essentially be approached from two angles – one physical, the other spiritual.

I will establish my covenant between me and thee (Abraham) and thy seed after thee in their generations for an everlasting covenant, to be a God unto thee, and to thy seed after thee. And I will give unto thee, and to thy seed after thee, the land wherein thou art a stranger, all the land of Canaan, for an everlasting possession; and I will be their God (Genesis 17:7–8).

In these verses we see God connecting his name with the descendants of Abraham (Hebrews) by particularly choosing them as well as promising the land of Canaan to the people. Underpinning it all is the fact that the covenant is everlasting. It will never be broken.

When we speak of the physical side of the covenant we are referring to the fact that God promised the land of Israel to God's people, the Hebrews (the Jews). Psalm 105 describes God's covenant with Israel:

He is the Lord our God: His judgments are in all the earth. He hath remembered his covenant for ever, the word which he commanded to a thousand generations. Which covenant he made with Abraham, and his oath unto Isaac; and confirmed the same unto Jacob for a law, and to Israel for an everlasting covenant: Saying, Unto thee will I give the land of Canaan, the lot of your inheritance... (Psalm 105: 7–11).

In Psalm 105 we are told that the people that God had chosen to be his own were given the land of Canaan, part of which is present day Israel. It was to be their inheritance, it was to be their portion, and the land was to be ever associated with the Hebrew or Jewish people.

The land of Israel and the Jewish people were to be inextricably linked. When the Jewish people were given back their homeland in 1948, this was a fulfilment of the promise that the land was to be an everlasting inheritance.

When we turn to the spiritual side of the covenant we find that God chose the Jewish people out of all nations. While it is true that a Jew can only be saved by faith, God set his choice first on the Jew.

The Bible makes it clear that not even the rebellion and disobedience of the Jews can terminate the covenant and the promises established through it. Indeed, it is prophesied that the Jews will return to the land of Israel in unbelief and only then will they be spiritually restored. Here we see the two sides of the covenant. The physical side is found in the Lord bringing back the Jews to the land in unbelief, while the spiritual side will finally be fulfilled when the Lord sanctifies them by cleansing them, giving them a new heart and giving them his Spirit:

> For I will take you from among the heathen, and gather you out of all countries, and will bring you into your own land. Then will I sprinkle clean water upon you, and ye shall be clean: from all your filthiness, and from all your idols, will I cleanse you. A new heart also will I give you, and a new spirit will I put within you: and I will take away the stony heart out of your flesh, and I will give you an heart of flesh. And I will put my spirit within you, and cause you to walk in my statutes, and ye shall keep my judgments, and do them. And ye shall dwell in the land that I gave to your fathers; and ye shall be my people, and I will be your God (Ezekiel 36:24–28).

Far from being rewarded for anything they have done, the Jews are blessed because God keeps his promises:

Therefore say unto the house of Israel, Thus saith the LORD God; I do not this for your sakes, O house of Israel, but for mine holy name's sake, which you have profaned among the heathen, whither ye went (Ezekiel 36:22).

The fact that God makes clear that the covenant he established with Israel was to be an everlasting one shows that God has not finished with Israel:

Thus saith the LORD, which giveth the sun for a light by day, and the ordinances of the moon and of the stars for a light by night, which divideth the sea when the waves thereof roar; the LORD of hosts is his name: if those ordinances depart from before me, saith the LORD, then the seed of Israel also shall cease from being a nation before me for ever (Jeremiah 31:35–36).

We are now left with the question which we posed at the beginning, namely, what does the weather we experience have to do with Israel? In the light of the covenant God makes with Israel, he also makes a promise that he will bless those who bless Israel and curse those who curse Israel:

Now the LORD had said unto Abram, Get thee out of thy country, and from thy kindred, and from thy father's house, unto a land that I will shew thee: and I will make of thee a great nation, and I will bless thee, and make thy name great; and thou shalt be a blessing: and I will bless them that bless thee, and curse him that curseth thee: and in thee shall all families of the earth be blessed (Genesis 12:1–3).

Blessed is he that blesseth thee, and cursed is he that curseth thee (Numbers 24:9).

If we attack the Jewish people we can only expect to be cursed. This is because they are beloved of the Lord, for he has chosen them to be objects of his mercy. However, at the same time, if we bless Israel as a nation, we too, may expect a blessing from God.

To attempt to separate the Jews from the land which God has given them is to come against the covenant that has been established for eternity. There are serious consequences for any people or nation that attempts to destroy the covenant established by God, consequences that will find its ultimate fulfilment at the end of this age.

For, behold, in those days, and in that time, when I shall bring again the captivity of Judah and Jerusalem, I will also gather all nations, and will bring them down into the valley of Jehoshaphat, and will plead with them there for my people and for my heritage Israel, whom they have scattered among the nations, and parted my land (Joel 3:2).

Here we see God promising finally to judge the nations at the end of the age for scattering the Jews and dividing the land of Israel. A similar prophecy is made in Zechariah.

And in that day will I make Jerusalem a burdensome stone for all people: all that burden themselves with it shall be cut in pieces, though all the people of the earth be gathered together against it (Zechariah 12:3).

These two passages make it clear that God does judge the nations for dividing the land of Israel.

However, we must remember that those who bless the Jewish people and Israel will in turn be blessed. If God blesses or curses in response to how the nations, in particular, treat the Jewish people, is it not possible that God would use the weather to both bless and to curse? If we divide the Land or attempt to rob the Jews of their inheritance should we not expect calamities to befall our nation?

13

Israel and God's Judgment of the Nations

We have already seen how Scripture makes clear that God has tied his name to the Jews and the land of Israel. In this chapter we will see how recent history testifies to the fact that God is angry with nations that have persecuted the Jews and tried to divide the land of Israel.

Britain and the Jewish homeland
Following the Second World War the British Government refused Jews who had survived the holocaust entry into Palestine. Instead they were imprisoned in camps in Cyprus. Canon Andrew White, former Envoy to the Middle East for the Archbishop of Canterbury, has commented that 'most British people are not even aware of the fact that we were taking Jews who had escaped Auschwitz and putting them in camps where many of them died in Cyprus.'[44] In the spring of 1947 Britain suffered perhaps her most severe winter on record. This was followed by dreadful flooding as the thawing snow combined with heavy rains. Britain was seen to be unmerciful to the Jews and therefore God poured forth his righteous judgment on her.

Ethiopian famine

The event that is etched most on people's minds from the 1980s is probably the severe famine which afflicted Ethiopia in 1984–85. Many years later the images are still easy to recall. Over a million people died as drought caused crops to fail and famine to take hold. Yet why would God afflict this nation so harshly? What had she done that had so angered the Lord?

We have seen how God has attached his name to the Jewish people by way of an eternal covenant. We also saw how God brought a severe famine that afflicted both Egypt and Canaan because they had persecuted Joseph, the Lord's anointed. It is only by looking at events in Ethiopia's history leading up to the famine that we are able to understand why God came in judgment against this land. At the same time, we will see that while God's anger was clearly shown, the famine was also the means of a glorious deliverance.

There has been a long history of Jews living in Ethiopia. Indeed, at one time they ruled the area of Ethiopia where they dwelt. However, in the twentieth century a number of events affected Ethiopia's relationship with the Jews. The most significant of these was the Yom Kippur war, as a result of which Ethiopia broke off all diplomatic relations with Israel, under threat from the Arab world. In 1977, Colonel Mengistu Haile Mariam became leader and the persecution of the Jews increased. Many were killed or made homeless. All had their land taken from them. In time Judaism was forbidden as was the teaching of Hebrew. It was clear that there was an orchestrated attempt to wipe out Judaism from Ethiopia.

What undoubtedly changed events was the famine which began in 1984. Ethiopia was forced to seek aid from the West and one of the countries that helped was Israel.

This enabled her to put pressure on Ethiopia on behalf of the Jews. Then, on November 18th, 1984, Operation Moses began which saw 8,000 Jews being rescued from Ethiopia and brought to Israel. The subsequent mission, Operation Joshua, saw 800 rescued. The famine had been the catalyst for the deliverance of many thousands of Jews.

Yet we should not forget that the famine was a judgment from God. The Ethiopian leaders had attempted to wipe out Judaism. They had persecuted the Jewish people which the word of God makes clear has serious consequences. God spoke and the land no longer brought forth its fruit. I am sure many people looked at the events of that time and asked why they were happening, but how many sought an answer from God? Did they look behind the scenes and see a nation that had broken God's commandments and persecuted his people?

In 2002 Ethiopia once more found herself in the grip of a dreadful famine. Again the link between God's judgment and persecution of God's people may be seen because, as *Prophecy Today* pointed out, 'The Ethiopian government has... actively encouraged the persecution of Christians, thousands of whom have been reduced to slavery or have suffered rape, torture and death. When a nation is led by corrupt and evil men it brings judgment upon the whole nation.'[45]

The perfect storm

In October 1991 an event took place on the coast of America that was described as the 'Perfect Storm'.

What was "perfect" about "The Perfect Storm"? Unusual circumstances allowed three weather systems to combine into one monster storm. Hurricane Grace, which had formed off the east coast of Florida on October 27th, weakened as it moved north and was downgraded to a tropical storm. About the same time, an extratropical cyclone developed over southern Canada, and a trailing cold front began to push across the Mid Atlantic States and New England. On October 29, the cold front caught up with the slower moving Grace. Wind shear from the surface front as well as winds aloft acted to tear Grace apart, but the extratropical cyclone absorbed much of her energy. On October 30, as the cyclone moved over warmer Gulf Stream waters it intensified into a super-storm with 100-foot waves and 80 mph winds. This new storm was not named at the time, so now it's referred to as the "Unnamed Hurricane of 1991." The "Perfect Storm" finally broke up over Nova Scotia, Canada, on the 2nd of November. Hybrid storms, such as this one are rare but can be particularly dangerous – some meteorologists say this was perhaps the worst North Atlantic storm in a century.[46]

As William Koenig has noted, this storm occurred at exactly the same time as the Madrid Conference was taking place. The USA and USSR were the conveners of the Conference which had as its purpose the establishment of bilateral talks between Israel and Syria, Lebanon and Jordan. The aim was to begin moves towards the establishment of a Palestinian state and the division of the land of Israel.[47] As we saw in the chapter on God's relationship with Israel there are serious consequences for any nation that attacks Israel or attempts to divide the land covenanted to her by God.

Hurricane Andrew

Less than a year later, in August 1992, Hurricane Andrew hit America. It was to become the most severe weather disaster ever to hit America as winds reached 177 mph. On August 23, the same day that Hurricane Andrew hit America, 'the Madrid Conference convened for the first time on American soil.'[48]

Road Map to peace

Up until 2002 it had been America who had been the chief negotiators when it came to bringing about a Palestinian state and a divided Promised Land. However, in that year things changed, when on April 10th 2002 the Quartet comprising America, the UN, EU and Russia was formed. Each would now work in co-operation. The EU and Russia in particular were now formally involved. After a meeting in New York City on July 16th the Quartet made a statement in which they reiterated their commitment to two states existing side by side. For Israel that would mean withdrawing to the pre-1967 borders.

It is in the light of this that we are able to understand the horrendous flooding that swept across Europe in the August of that year. Across Europe dozens died, thousands were affected and damage ran into billions of Euros. Russia was also particularly badly affected.

2003 is also a year that will long remain in the memories of people across Europe. A severe heat-wave engulfed the continent leading to thousands of deaths. Yet why did it happen? Scientists were unable to give any concrete explanation. However, when we look at events from a spiritual perspective, it becomes clear. It was at this time that the 'Road Map to Peace' was presented by the Quartet

(UN, EU, US and Russia). Now it was not just America who was putting pressure on Israel to give up land, but Europe as well. God's judgment was immediate and direct. The day after the Road Map was presented to the leaders of Israel and the Palestinians, tornadoes began sweeping across America. In the space of eleven days 412 tornadoes were recorded. However, as has already been mentioned, Europe was to suffer as well. The heat-wave that spread across Europe had a catastrophic effect. Thousands died, billions of pounds were lost as a result of crop failure and rivers dried up. Other parts of the world were also suffering from the heat-wave, while some places were experiencing hailstones large enough to puncture holes in roofs. Some scientists pointed to global warming. However, when we understand that God is sovereign and is in control of all things we realise that the events of the summer of 2003 had something far more significant behind them. God was communicating to the world. The nations were attempting defiantly to carve up his land. God was responding by cursing the earth. Yet once more we should be thankful that his mercy was evident in that he kept his promise that he would not destroy the earth.

Hurricane Katrina

As has been seen, on one level Hurricane Katrina must be seen in the light of God's judgment on the city of New Orleans. The immorality prevalent there could not go on forever with God remaining silent, and through the flooding God spoke. However, on another level the hurricane that swept through New Orleans was in response to what America was, at that precise moment, doing to Israel. On August 23, 2005 President Bush spoke these words:

...I want to congratulate Prime Minister Sharon for having made a very tough decision. As I said in my remarks yesterday in Salt Lake City, the Prime Minister made a courageous decision to withdraw from the Gaza.[49]

It was on this day that the last remaining Jews were forced out of Samaria. On the very same day Hurricane Katrina began forming. On 24th it was declared to be a Tropical Storm and given the name Katrina, on 25th it became a hurricane and on 26th the hurricane swept over Florida.

The parallels between what happened in Israel as a result of the force put on her by America and what happened in America as a result of the force of Hurricane Katrina are detailed by William Koenig. I will list a few which are particularly graphic.

On August 17, Israeli Prime Minister Ariel Sharon authorized the mandatory evacuation of residents refusing to evacuate Gaza.

On September 7, an hour after New Orleans Mayor Ray Nagin ordered, by force if necessary, mandatory evacuation of the crippled city, soldiers began coaxing some of Katrina's holdouts from their homes due to fire or disease risks.

Nine thousand Israelis were evicted by their government. Shortly thereafter, one million Americans were evicted by Hurricane Katrina.

Israeli security teams went from home to home to evict Israelis. So also teams of soldiers went from home to home in New Orleans evicting people.

Buses took Israelis out of Gaza and northern Samaria to their temporary homes, as did buses take

New Orleans residents to their temporary homes in Texas and other southern states.

While 2,700 homes were demolished in Gaza and 300 homes in northern Samaria, 225,000 homes were demolished in the Southern U.S., with many more severely damaged.[50]

Tornado hits London

On 7th December 2006, Prime Minister Tony Blair stood next to President George Bush in Washington and declared that he would be travelling to the Middle-East 'soon'. The purpose of his visit would be to speed up the peace process between Israel and the Palestinians. The very same day a tornado hit London, England. Blair's declaration that once more he was planning to put pressure on Israel to divide her land brought a response from heaven.[51]

Further attempts to divide the Land

On 18th January 2007 U.S. Secretary of State Condoleezza Rice went to Germany and met with Chancellor Merkel and together they declared that there was the definite prospect of progress on the Road Map to a two-state solution, with Israel and the Palestinians dwelling side by side. Rice had just been on a tour of the Middle East and the plan was for the Quartet to convene on February 2nd to deal with the future of Israel and Palestine. The next day Condoleezza Rice went to London to meet with Prime Minister Tony Blair to talk with him about the Middle East problem.

While Condoleezza Rice was in Germany there was a great storm so severe that she left early so that she would be able to get to London. On the day she was talking with Tony Blair about the Road Map the storm hit Britain. The headline on *The Times* website that day was *Winds and Hain make storm for Condi visit.*[52] How extraordinary that it should unknowingly point to the link between Condoleezza Rice's visit and the storm. The article went on to say:

> Condoleezza Rice flew into stormy weather today as she arrived in London for the last leg of her visit to the Middle East and Europe.
>
> The US Secretary of State first had to endure a rough landing as her aircraft touched down in winds gusting to 80mph (130kph), before heading to Whitehall for meetings with Tony Blair and Margaret Beckett, the Foreign Secretary, that are expected to be made awkward by an outspoken attack on the Bush Administration by their Cabinet colleague, Peter Hain.[53]

At least fourteen people were killed as winds reached 99mph during the course of the day. In Germany the winds reached 122mph and resulted in the deaths of at least ten people.

The Quartet did meet on February 2nd as arranged. The result was a tornado in Florida. The Independent newspaper reported it like this:

> A dusk-to-dawn curfew remained in effect in parts of central Florida last night in the wake of furious thunderstorms and at least one tornado that raked the state on Friday, leaving 20 people dead and flattening hundreds of houses and mobile homes.
>
> ...In Volusia County alone, executives calculated, as many as 500 properties had been hit, causing at least $80m (£40m) in damage.
>
> The storm was one of the worst in Florida's history.[54]

It is hoped that by pointing the reader to just a few significant events in recent history, it has become clear how God does judge the nations when they attempt to divide the land of Israel. Certainly many more examples could be cited. What I would urge the reader to do is observe how, when pressure is put on Israel to cede land, storms quickly follow, often on the same day.

14

Can Satan Control the Weather?

Satan and his work

Satan was once an angel who dwelt in the presence of God. He, like the other angels, would have worshipped the Lord round the throne. Yet in trying to make himself equal with God, Satan was cast out of heaven. At the Cross, Jesus died not only for the sins of mankind, but also in order that the works of the evil one should be destroyed. If Satan is now defeated, what is it that he is able to do?

We perhaps find the greatest insight into what Satan is able to do by looking at the titles given to Satan. The name Satan means *adversary* or *enemy* and speaks of him as being in direct opposition to the purposes and plans of God and to God himself. He is variously described as a deceiver, a liar, a tempter, the prince of this world and Beelzebub. His great purpose is to deceive the people of earth so that they might remain blind to the things of God:

> In whom the god of this world hath blinded the minds of them which believe not, lest the light of the glorious gospel of Christ, who is the image of God, should shine unto them (II Corinthians 4:4).

Satan's work is not confined to the unbeliever but also extends to the believer. His desire is to cause the believer to fall into sin and to live a defeated life: 'your adversary the devil, as a roaring lion, walketh about, seeking whom he may devour' (I Peter 5:8). Yet the Christian has been provided with all the armour necessary to thwart the works of the Devil, for he has been placed into Christ who is his shield, breastplate and armour. Moreover, God has provided the Christian with the Holy Spirit, by whom he is able to walk in holiness before the Lord and resist the Devil's attacks.

Though Satan is able to attack the Christian and blind the non-Christian, it is God who is still in control. Everything was created for him and is subject to him and nothing Satan does can change that fact:

> For by him were all things created, that are in heaven, and that are in earth, visible and invisible, whether they be thrones, or dominions, or principalities, or powers: all things were created by him, and for him (Colossians 1:16).

Satan as the prince of the air

We are now in a position to begin examining whether Satan is able directly to control the weather. We might surmise from Ephesians that Satan is able to control the weather.

> Wherein in time past ye walked according to the course of this world, according to the prince of the power of the air, the spirit that now worketh in the children of disobedience... (Ephesians 2:2).

If he is the ruler of the air it might follow that he is able to control the weather. However, this is to misunderstand what it means for Satan to be the prince of the air. The context makes clear that it is relating to Satan's influence in the world over unbelievers:

> ...the spirit that now worketh in the children of disobedience.

These words explain the work of the prince of the power of the air. From this verse alone we cannot say that Satan is given the power to affect the weather since it does not mention the weather. We would have to make a giant leap to get from Satan as prince of the air influencing unbelievers to Satan being in control of the elements.

Satan and Job

It is in the Book of Job that we have the only explicit mention of Satan in connection with the weather. However, even here we have to be careful that we do not suggest Satan has powers or abilities which he does not have.

The Book of Job opens with Satan coming before God, arguing that the only reason Job is faithful to God is because he has put a hedge of protection round him. God in response says:

> Behold, all that [Job] hath is in thy power; only upon himself put not forth thine hand. So Satan went forth from the presence of the LORD (Job 1:12).

There then follows a record of the sufferings of Job, including the loss of his oxen, sheep and camels and the death of almost all his servants. However, what is particularly relevant to our study is the way in which Job's sons die:

> ...there came also another (servant), and said, Thy sons and thy daughters were eating and drinking wine in their eldest brother's house: and, behold, there came a great wind from the wilderness, and smote the four corners of the house, and it fell upon the young men, and they are dead; and I only am escaped alone to tell thee (Job 1:18–19).

Bearing in mind that God has put all that Job owns into the hands of Satan it seems right to assume that the wind was caused by Satan. If this is the case it would seem as though we would have to conclude that God is not in control of all weather. What is more, we would have to say that, at least on occasions, Satan has power over the weather.

However, a number of verses suggest that it is not as simple as that. Firstly, immediately following the death of Job's sons as a result of the great wind we find Job going before the Lord in worship:

> Naked came I out of my mother's womb, and naked shall I return thither: the LORD gave, and the LORD hath taken away; blessed be the name of the LORD (Job 1:21).

Here Job attributes all that he previously had to the gracious provision of the Lord and gives him thanks. At the same time, he acknowledges that the taking away of his goods and children is the Lord's doing. We might conclude that Job is being pious at best, or at worst attributing to

God something which was really Satan's doing. However, neither is the case for the word of God goes on to say:

> In all this Job sinned not, nor charged God foolishly (Job 1:22).

If Job had accused God of doing something that was the work of Satan we would rightly expect that the word of God would say that Job had sinned and charged God foolishly. However, the Bible makes it clear that he did neither. Therefore, from this verse alone we are able to conclude that Job's afflictions were ultimately ordained by God.

In the fullness of time Job's possessions are restored to him and his friends and family gather to comfort him:

> Then came there unto him all his brethren, and all his sisters, and all they that had been of his acquaintance before, and did eat bread with him in his house: and they bemoaned him, and comforted him over all the evil that the LORD had brought upon him: every man also gave him a piece of money, and every one an earring of gold (Job 42:11).

Once again we are told that the evil that had befallen Job had come from the hand of the Lord. As Isaiah says; 'The LORD creates evil' (Isaiah 45:7). It should be pointed out that the word for 'evil' in the Hebrew may just as easily be translated 'calamity'.

It would certainly seem as though Satan is responsible for the calamities that befall Job, yet at the same time there are verses that clearly point to the hand of the Lord behind it all.

Throughout the Bible there is evidence that God uses

evil men and evil spirits to do his bidding. In the Book of Judges it is recorded that:

> God sent an evil spirit between Abimelech and the men of Shechem ... (Judges 9:23).

On another occasion Scripture records:

> And the evil spirit from the LORD was upon Saul, as he sat in his house with his javelin in his hand (I Samuel 19:9).

Therefore, it should not surprise us when we find that God uses Satan to fulfil his purposes. On one level it is true that Satan attacks Job, however we must remember that any power Satan has is given to him by God. What is more, without God's express permission he could not use the power granted him. However, the Bible goes beyond even the idea that God somehow allowed Satan to act, for this might suggest some reluctance on God's part. Rather, God was ultimately the ordainer of Job's loss and so was ultimately the cause of the wind's coming and destroying the house where his sons were feasting.

Perhaps we might draw upon an illustration to explain the cause of the storm that resulted in the death of Job's sons. If I were to take hold of a stick and use it to hit something one might easily say that it was the stick that hit the object. However, the stick is just the tool in my hand. God used Satan to fulfil his purposes. Just as a king is God's servant and God can turn his heart whichever way he chooses,[55] so he controls Satan and is able to use him to bring about his purposes. Therefore, we are able to say that while it is true that Satan caused the wind, it is also true that Satan was merely doing the will of God.

In saying this, we might want to reflect on why Job suffered such loss. The opening verses of the book clearly testify that he was upright and perfect:

> There was a man in the land of Uz, whose name was Job; and that man was perfect and upright, and one that feared God, and eschewed evil (Job 1:1).

However, when Job comes face to face with God after all his friends have addressed him, we see him suddenly aware of his true nature:

> Behold, I am vile; what shall I answer thee? I will lay mine hand upon my mouth. ...I have heard of thee by the hearing of the ear: but now mine eye seeth thee. Wherefore I abhor myself, and repent in dust and ashes (Job 40:4, 42:5–6).

It is true that Job is earlier described as 'perfect'. However, we must understand what it means to have a perfect heart. David Wilkerson explains it in the following way:

> To come to grips with the idea of perfection, we first must understand that perfection does not mean a sinless, flawless existence. People judge by outward appearance, by what they see. But God judges the heart, the unseen motives (I Samuel 16:7). David had a perfect heart toward God 'all the days of his life' – yet David failed the Lord often. In fact, his life was marked forever by adultery and a notorious murder.
>
> No, perfection in the Lord's eyes means something entirely different. ...It means to finish what has been

started, to make a complete performance. John Wesley called this concept of perfection 'constant obedience'; that is, a perfect heart is a responsive heart, one that answers quickly and totally all the Lord's wooing, whisperings and warnings. Such a heart says at all times, 'Speak, Lord, for Your servant is listening. Show me the path, and I will walk in it.'[56]

Job's heart was searchable, but in and of himself there was no good thing. The loss that Job suffered was to show him his true nature. It was only once he saw God's greatness and his own vileness that he could be restored. God had brought the many afflictions against Job in order that he might see the greatness of God and his own wretchedness. As Job humbles himself beneath the mighty hand of the Lord we see him exalted and blessed.

It is true that Satan has power over the unbeliever, and is able to attack the believer. However, he can do nothing unless the Lord permits him and he certainly has no influence over the elements unless the Lord grants him the power in order that God's purposes might be fulfilled.

15

Why Doesn't God always Judge?

When the Bible makes it so clear that a nation which disobeys God will be punished by floods, drought, pestilence or the sword it might seem strange that God doesn't afflict the world more. Normally, we hear the question, *why does God allow disasters?*, yet in the light of what has already been said, a more appropriate question might be, *why don't we see more disasters?* Surely, as we look around the world we could each list countries that we think deserve God's judgment, including our own, and certainly deserve it as much as any other nation. However, there are a number of issues that this fails to recognise.

First, the fact that God does not always judge a nation, even though she deserves it, points to the mercy of God. We are aware of the mercy of God with regard the individual: though we each deserve his wrath, God 'is longsuffering to us-ward, not willing that any should perish, but that all should come to repentance' (II Peter 3:9). Equally, God's longsuffering extends to nations.

Second, every calamity should not only be seen as a judgment upon the nation or place involved, but should also act as a warning to others looking on.

Third, God responds to a praying people. We are not always aware of the intercession that is taking place on behalf of a nation by certain individuals.

The mercy of God

When we are chastised we might ask why someone else isn't chastised as well. When another nation suffers horrific calamity we may wonder why God's judgment was so severe when other nations go free. However, we must begin by realising that everything God does is just. God in his very nature is just and it is impossible for God to do anything against his nature. This should lead us to acknowledge that when God judges he does so with perfect justice.

We also need to realise that God is merciful in his dealings with the world. We see that clearly expressed in the Noahic covenant, for here God declares that he has observed the nature of mankind that it is wicked. None of us deserves to be alive. We only deserve God's judgment, and no nation deserves God's favour. Therefore, the fact that neither the whole earth nor a nation is utterly wiped out is a testimony to the mercy of God. When God's judgment is severe against a nation we must remember that it is only the mercy of God that restrains God from meting out his full anger upon the people.

A nation that deserves judgment from God may experience that judgment delayed. Consider how the people of Judah were taken into exile during the reign of Jehoiakim as recorded in Daniel. However, II Kings 24:3, 4 tells us that this happened because of the sins of Mannasseh. There were three kings who reigned between Mannasseh and Jehoiakim. God did not act immediately, but ultimately he judged the people. Just because a nation is not being judged by God does not mean that it is living righteously:

it may simply be experiencing the mercy of God with the purpose that it might repent of its sin. However, failure to repent will lead to its being judged in God's time.

In the light of our consideration of the mercy of God it is worth mentioning a verse in Matthew that relates directly to this:

> For he maketh his sun to rise on the evil and on the good, and sendeth rain on the just and on the unjust (Matthew 5:45b).

It is certainly possible that we might read this verse and conclude that God does not use the elements to judge. Taken at face value and out of context it would seem as though Jesus is saying just that, since we are told that both the just and the unjust receive the blessing of the sun and the rain. This would appear to contradict much of what we have already found to be the case from Scripture; that sin and 'natural disasters' are directly related. However, when we consider the context within which this statement is made we realise that Jesus is speaking about the mercy of God:

> Ye have heard that it hath been said, Thou shalt love thy neighbour, and hate thine enemy. But I say unto you, Love your enemies, bless them that curse you, do good to them that hate you, and pray for them which despitefully use you, and persecute you; that ye may be the children of your Father which is in heaven: for he maketh his sun to rise on the evil and on the good, and sendeth rain on the just and on the unjust. (Matthew 5:43–45).

Jesus is pointing to the benevolence of God. God's provision of both sun and rain is testimony to his mercy, love and goodness, not just to the good, but to the wicked as well. Jesus is not saying that the wicked are not judged; rather he is saying both the wicked and the righteous experience the goodness of God.

Far from the verses in Matthew contradicting the clear link between sin and judgment, they merely point to the fact that though floods and drought and the like are always sent in response to sin, their absence does not necessarily testify to a nation's goodness. The wicked may still experience the mercies of God. Rather than God's goodness being only in response to the humility and righteousness of a nation, it may on occasions be that it is a testimony to the patience of the Lord. When we see the sun rise in the morning, when we see his wonderful provision of rain, we should look up to the Lord and give thanks. When we see the mercy of God it should lead us to repent. This is expressed wonderfully in the words of the Apostle Paul:

> Or despisest thou the riches of his goodness and forbearance and longsuffering; not knowing that the goodness of God leadeth thee to repentance? (Romans 2:4).

A warning to others

When a nation is experiencing the mercy of God she should look upon those nations that have suffered the judgment of God and consider her ways. As the Bible makes clear, failure to do so will lead to a similar judgment falling upon that people:

> There were present at that season some that told him of the Galilaeans, whose blood Pilate had mingled with

their sacrifices. And Jesus answering them, Suppose ye that these Galilaeans were sinners above all the Galilaeans, because they suffered such things? I tell you, Nay: but, except ye repent, ye shall all likewise perish. Or those eighteen, upon whom the tower in Siloam fell, and slew them, think ye that they were sinners above all men that dwelt in Jerusalem? I tell you, Nay: but, except ye repent, ye shall all likewise perish (Luke 13:2-5).

In the verses just quoted we see the direct link between calamity and the judgment of God against sin. Those who have not yet experienced calamity are warned that if they do not repent they too will perish. Some might say that the passage denies the link between calamity and the judgment of God since the Galilaeans and 'the eighteen' suffered greatly yet were not worse sinners. However, the verse does not deny that they were sinners and deserved judgment. Neither does it say that they were not judged. In fact it says the opposite. In speaking of those yet to repent, Jesus warns them that they *too* shall perish if they do not repent. They are called to look on those people who have been judged and take heed by repenting.

Intercession

Finally, throughout the Bible it is recorded how God responds to the prayers of his people. He delivers them from the enemy, saves them from captivity, and protects them in the midst of suffering. It is also evident that God turns from punishing his people when they turn to him in repentance. We have seen how God, in his mercy, has answered the cries of the people in the midst of affliction, drought and war. When people humble themselves beneath the mighty hand of God and cry out to God, he answers in mercy and loving kindness.

It must be wondered how many times God has been merciful as a result of certain people joining together, perhaps in secret, to petition the Lord for his mercy upon their nation. Consider how God was *willing* to save Sodom for the sake of a handful of righteous people. Is it not the case that God is willing to do the same in our day? We need to see the events that happen daily with spiritual eyes. The earnest supplications of a humble heart reach heaven. Elijah was a 'man of like passions such as we', we are told, and he caused the heavens to be closed and then to open (James 5:17–18). He had no power in and of himself, but his prayers were powerful.

God does judge, yet his judgment is always tempered by mercy. The prayers of the righteous, even the presence of the righteous, can cause the Lord to withhold his anger. However, there are also times when God is merciful simply to lead a nation back to himself.

16

Is 'Science' Wrong?

The scientific world is currently very outspoken on the subject of Global Warming and Climate Change. Bearing in mind all that has been written so far it is necessary for us to look at some of the pronouncements made by proponents of the Global Warming Hypothesis.

Global warming and climate change
'In common usage, 'global warming' often refers to the warming that can occur as a result of increased emissions of greenhouse gases from human activities.'[57] This is closely associated with climate change. It is argued that as a result of the warming of the oceans and atmosphere the climate will change resulting in more severe weather.

What about observable evidence?

The seasons
Those who believe in global warming frequently argue that one of the main pieces of observable evidence of global

warming is the changing nature of the seasons. They would point to the fact that spring is arriving earlier. Indeed, it is even suggested that we are seeing the end of seasons with one season merging into another. Tearfund, a Christian action organisation, produced a pamphlet, subtitled, *Living responsibly in a world of climate change*.[58] In this the writers urge the reader to make a positive change to the way they live in the light of climate change. One of the arguments they point to for the existence of climate change caused by man-made global warming is the changing seasons. Referring to the climate in Honduras as an example, they report that 'nowadays it's difficult to distinguish between summer and winter.'[59] Closer to home a recent Europe-wide study discovered that spring is beginning earlier, while autumn is later.[60]

It may well be true that we are currently witnessing seasonal changes. Certainly there is plenty of evidence to suggest this to be the case. However, the issue is not really whether we are experiencing changes in the seasons, but rather what is the cause when changes in the seasons take place. In recent times we have been led to believe that man-made global warming is the cause. However, whatever scientists might say we must take as our final authority the word of God. This is very clear on the matter. Following the Flood, God made a covenant through Noah that:

> While the earth remaineth, seedtime and harvest, and cold and heat, and summer and winter, and day and night shall not cease (Genesis 8:22).

God promised that there will be no end to seasons. If God has declared it, we can rest assured that he will faithfully fulfil his word. Therefore we can say that though the seasons might lengthen or shorten, they will remain for we are told that 'summer and winter… shall not cease.' Neither will 'seedtime and harvest' which are directly associated with the seasons. While it is true that certain countries may go through periods of time without seedtime or harvest, the *earth* as a whole will never do so.

When we turn to the Book of Daniel we discover that while the seasons may remain they do change:

> And he changeth the times and the seasons… (Daniel 2:21).

It is God who is the author of the seasons, it is God who causes the seasons to continue to exist and it is God who changes the seasons. We can look for so-called 'natural causes' as to why we are seeing change in the seasons but ultimately it is God who is in control. God has his purposes in all things and he will bring them about.

Extreme weather

The second great piece of evidence usually put forward for the existence of man-made global warming is the increase in extreme weather conditions. Climatologists point to the fact that we are experiencing more floods and droughts and greater severity of storms.

Scientists stress that recent weather events prove that man is causing the climate to change by causing the earth to warm up:

> For example, in recent years massive storms and subsequent floods have hit China, Italy, England, Korea, Bangladesh, Venezuela, and Mozambique. In England in 2000, floods classified as 'once in 30-year events'

occurred twice in the same month. Moreover, the winter of 2000/1 was the wettest six months recorded in Britain since records began in the 18th century, while in the summer of 2003 Britain recorded the first ever temperature of 100°F since records began. ...There is also evidence that more storms are occurring in the northern hemisphere.[61]

In an earlier chapter we concluded that it is God who actively sends floods, droughts and storms. However, having said that, could it be that God is sending these climatic disasters in response to our excessive use of fossil fuels?

Ken Ham has written that 'the development of energy sources, the mining of mineral resources, the cutting of timber for building, etc., is not wrong. Ecclesiastes 3:1–8 states that there is a time to plant and a time to uproot, a time to kill and a time to heal, a time to tear down and a time to build, a time to keep and a time to throw away, a time for war and a time for peace.'[62] If there is a sin that is connected to our treatment of the planet then it is our greed and idolatry: putting possessions and worldly pleasures before God. It is not wrong to drive a car, fly by plane, clear trees to build houses. Indeed, the Bible makes it plain that the use of an abundance of trees to build the temple was not wrong, neither was it wrong to cut down trees for the purposes of war. However, when these things arise out of greed, idolatry and covetousness then it is sin. If God is judging us for our behaviour then these would be the things that God would deal with. It is not a matter of reaching a point in our use of fossil fuels where we overstep the mark. Rather, it is our motive that matters.

Ice-caps

The ice-caps of Antarctica and the Arctic have come under particular investigation in the light of recent studies of global warming. It is argued that the ice-caps are fast disappearing as a result of man-made global warming. However, the Bible says it is God who creates and sends the ice and snow. God asks Job, 'where does the ice and frost come?' The clear implication is that God brings the ice:

> Out of whose womb came the ice? and the hoary frost of heaven, who hath gendered it? (Job 38:29).

The psalmist similarly declares that God 'casteth forth his ice like morsels' (Psalm 147:17).

Other verses point to the fact that snow comes from God:

> For he saith to the snow, Be thou on the earth... (Job 37:6).
> He giveth snow like wool... (Psalm 147:16).
> Snow... fulfil(s) his word (Psalm 148:8).

If it is God who brings the snow and ice, it is surely true that the ice-caps are his creation and his work. It is also logical that if he wants to melt them, then that is his to do as well. Again Job says, 'Drought and heat consume the snow waters' (Job 24:19). God's word reveals to us that drought and heat come from God: he must therefore be the one who causes the snow and ice to melt.

What then is causing the changes to the climate?

Two things that have a significant bearing on our weather are water vapour and clouds. Water vapour is a 'natural', as opposed to a man-made, greenhouse gas and causes the globe to further warm up by amplifying the effect of the warming of the earth. As the atmosphere becomes warmer the water vapour increases. The water vapour traps some of the solar energy that radiates back from the earth, stopping it from escaping from the atmosphere. This causes the earth and lower atmosphere to become even warmer. Thus we see that water vapour plays an important part in determining the climate we experience.

Psalm 148 tells us that it is God who controls water vapour, which obeys his command:

> Fire, and hail; snow, and vapour; stormy wind fulfil[s] his word (Psalm 148:8).

Since water vapour has a direct effect on the climate, if God controls the vapour, the climate is also under his sway.

With regard clouds, the Bible-believing Christian is able to say with confidence that it is God who forms them:

> He bindeth up the waters in his thick clouds... (Job 26:8).

> He had commanded the clouds from above...
> (Psalm 78:23).

It is widely recognised that clouds have a direct impact on the temperature of the earth:

> Clouds are able to both heat and cool the planet. They cause warming by acting as a blanket, reducing the amount of surface heat radiated into space. Estimates are that clouds warm the earth by about 9°F. In a reverse

way clouds also absorb incoming sunlight and reflect it back into space, preventing it from warming the earth. It is thought that this reduces surface temperatures by about 22°F. Thus it appears that clouds have a net cooling effect.[63]

The fact that clouds have such an important part to play in determining our climate shows once more that it is God who controls the weather. If God brings the clouds into existence, as the Bible makes plain he does, it is evident that it is God who regulates the temperatures across the earth.

Do we conclude from this that man has no effect on the environment?

The problem with the argument that carbon emissions from human activities are causing global warming is that 'Nature' and Man are the starting point and there is no recognition of God who is sovereign. If we start from the belief that God controls the sun, water vapour, clouds and the weather it is possible we would come to very different conclusions.

A particular problem facing those who believe the Bible to be the word of God whilst also maintaining that the earth is warming due to man-made carbon emissions is the increase in water vapour in the atmosphere. Proponents of man-made global warming argue that between the years 1900 and 2000 the temperature of the earth has increased by 0.6°C, of which 0.2°C is directly attributable to carbon emissions. They go on to argue that the remaining 0.4°C is due to the increase in water vapour that has been caused by the temperature increase resulting from increases in CO_2 in the atmosphere.[64] However, as we have already seen, the

Bible says that God controls the water vapour. That is to say, man does not determine increases and decreases in water vapour. Therefore, 0.4°C of the total 0.6°C increase has definitely arisen because of God. However, that still leaves us with the question: scientifically, what has caused an increase in water vapour? In order to answer this question faithfully while holding to the Bible's assertion that God controls the water vapour, we need to look for something that would cause the earth's temperature to rise, and so cause the water vapour to increase, but which is not attributable to man.

It is here that we can turn to a theory put forward recently that proposes that it is the sun which is to blame. While this theory is still under scrutiny it fits in well with what the Bible says.

It has been demonstrated that when stars explode they emit cosmic rays. On reaching the earth's atmosphere the rays produce electrically charged particles. 'These particles attract water molecules from the air and cause them to clump together until they condense into clouds.'[65] The amount of cosmic rays reaching the atmosphere is determined primarily by how magnetically active the sun is. Consequently, a more active (brighter) sun leads to fewer rays reaching the earth and so fewer low-level clouds are formed. Since low-level clouds have a cooling effect on the earth, fewer clouds will have a warming effect. In the last century we have seen a more active sun, demonstrated by an increase in sunspots. The result has been fewer clouds. Thus the earth has been warming up. Historical records have shown the direct correlation between the strength of the magnetic shield of the sun and temperatures.[66]

The Bible clearly states that the stars belong to God; therefore when they explode they are under the direction of God (Psalm 8:3). Second, we have seen that the sun is under God's control. The activity of the sun has been seen to determine the clouds. Finally, we have seen that God makes the clouds. The three ingredients that are making a significant contribution to the warming of the planet are each explicitly said to be under God's control.

In addition to this, during the 1960s and early 1970s there was a period of cooling. It was for that reason that scientists at the time thought we were about to enter an ice age. Significantly, during this period, the sun was less active. This still leaves the question, don't carbon emissions have some affect on the temperature of the earth?

First, let us remember that even the IPCC states that only 0.2°C of the temperature increase in the twentieth century was directly attributable to carbon emissions. However, we have seen that it has been suggested that due to the sun's being more active the earth has been warming up. Therefore, during the twentieth century, the increase in temperature caused directly by carbon emissions must have been significantly below 0.2°C. However, if CO_2 does cause temperatures to rise, even a tiny amount of temperature increase due to carbon emissions might be seen as a sign that God is not in total control of the weather.

To answer this, we have to understand the relationship between the oceans and CO_2. When the temperature of the oceans warm up they release CO_2 into the atmosphere. This is why we are seeing temperatures and atmospheric CO_2 rising concurrently. The sun is causing both to rise. Research by Lance Endersbee shows this to be the case:

Comparing satellite temperature data over the past 21 years to the measured level of CO_2 at the state-of-the art laboratory at Mauna Loa, Endersbee shows an almost perfect correlation of atmospheric CO_2 to sea surface temperature. As the activity of the Sun had caused a warming of the ocean surface over that period, it was no surprise that atmospheric CO_2 tended to increase. A period of reduced solar activity, which we appear to be entering, will allow the oceans to cool, causing a reduction in atmospheric carbon dioxide.[67]

After all that has been said, we must return to the Bible, for there we find that God is the ultimate agent of any changes to our climate. Any warming (or cooling) of the planet is due to the specific intervention of the Lord.

17

The Environment and the End-times

In this chapter we will consider some of the climatic catastrophes that will occur at the end of the age. This chapter will not deal with the end-times in detail, although certain observations will be made. With this in mind we will begin by turning to Matthew 24, a key passage in understanding the unfolding of events in the last days.

> And Jesus went out, and departed from the temple: and his disciples came to him for to shew him the buildings of the temple.
>
> And Jesus said unto them, See ye not all these things? Verily I say unto you, There shall not be left here one stone upon another, that shall not be thrown down.
>
> And as he sat upon the mount of Olives, the disciples came unto him privately, saying, Tell us, when shall these things be? And what shall be the sign of thy coming, and of the end of the world?
>
> And Jesus answered and said unto them, Take heed that no man deceive you. For many shall come in my name, saying, I am Christ; and shall deceive many. And

ye shall hear of wars and rumours of wars: see that
ye be not troubled: for all these things must come to
pass, but the end is not yet. For nation shall rise against
nation, and kingdom against kingdom: and there shall
be famines, and pestilences, and earthquakes, in divers
places. All these are the beginning of sorrows (Matthew
24:1–8).

A careful comparison of this passage with the associated
one in Luke 21 makes it clear that in Matthew, Jesus is
speaking about the end of the age. (For an analysis of this
see endnote[68].) Therefore, we may conclude that 'famine,
and pestilences, and earthquakes in divers places' (Matthew
24:7) will take place in the end-times. This is significant
since it clearly points to the fact that nothing mankind does
will prevent these things from happening. These events are
given to warn the believer that the end is near. They are
sent by God in order that we might lift up our heads and
see that our 'redemption draweth nigh' (Luke 21:28).

In a parallel passage in Revelation it is recorded how the
Lord opens the seals. When the sixth seal is opened the
following is described:

And I beheld when he had opened the sixth seal, and,
lo, there was a great earthquake; and the sun became
black as sackcloth of hair, and the moon became as
blood; and the stars of heaven fell unto the earth, even
as a fig tree casteth her untimely figs, when she is
shaken of a mighty wind (Revelation 6:12–13).

Following these events, at the very end of the age, there will
be calamities on a scale that the world has not previously
seen. These are described as the wrath of God (Revelation

16:1), something which the believer won't experience. It is the judgment of God against mankind. The seventh seal will be opened and there will be silence in heaven which will be followed by

Voices, and thunderings, and lightnings, and an earthquake. And the seven angels which had the seven trumpets prepared themselves to sound. The first angel sounded, and there followed hail and fire mingled with blood, and they were cast upon the earth: and the third part of trees was burnt up, and all green grass was burnt up (Revelation 8:5–7).

Finally Revelation 16 records the 'seven last plagues.' What follows is just a part of what is described:

And the fourth angel poured out his vial upon the sun; and power was given unto him to scorch men with fire. And men were scorched with great heat... And there were voices, and thunders, and lightnings; and there was a great earthquake, such as was not since men were upon the earth, so mighty an earthquake, and so great. ...And there fell upon men a great hail out of heaven, every stone about the weight of a talent: and men blasphemed God because of the plague of the hail; for the plague thereof was exceeding great (Revelation 16:8–9, 18, 21).

In referring to various parts of Revelation, it is hoped that the reader has seen something of what is prophesied for the climax of this age. Certainly, at the centre will be great climatic change and catastrophe. No matter what man tries to do, nothing will prevent that which the Lord has declared will occur. In saying that, we should not come to the conclusion that these merely prove that God knows the future. They are there to show us that he is in control, and all these events are the result of the hand of the Lord. The famines and other calamities are God's response to the wickedness in the world.

18

A Message to the Church

In the light of all that has been said so far, we must ask, How does this relate to the Church? I believe there are four areas in the life of the Church that should be affected. The first I would term the *ministry of the prophetic*. By this I mean the role the church has in warning people of God's impending judgment and of explaining what God is doing at any given time in the life of a nation. This will lead naturally to a call for a nation experiencing God's judgment to repent and for one knowing God's blessing to give thanks. The second ministry the church has been given is that of intercessory prayer. The church has been called to seek the Lord for his mercy and to plead on behalf of others. Third, the Lord has sent the Church out to bear testimony to him and to point people to the One who is the way of salvation. (This book should radically alter the answers we give to some of the questions posed by non-Christians.) Finally, and perhaps most importantly, it should bring us closer to a correct understanding of God, his ways and his purposes. This in turn should lead us to exalt him in our lives and realise our own unworthiness before him.

The Church has been given a vital role in being God's spokesman, proclaiming the oracles of God. This is an awesome and grave work that we have been called to. Yet far too often we have abdicated our responsibility. However, if we do so we are no better than Jonah, who, having been given a message to give to the people of Nineveh, headed for Tarshish. We are called to enter into the courts of the Lord, to hear his word and to proclaim it from the rooftops. The word of God tells us that God always forewarns us when he is going to judge:

> Surely the LORD God will do nothing, but he revealeth his secret unto his servants the prophets (Amos 3:7).

Therefore, when he is about to visit in judgment, we must be those who hear his voice and warn the people. As the mouthpiece of God, it is the Church's burden to call upon the nation to forsake her wickedness and turn to the Lord.

There are times when God must judge particular nations because of their own unwillingness to yield to him, and in order that his justice might be displayed. It is in the midst of judgment that the Church within the land must rise up and call for the nation to repent:

> Therefore also now, saith the LORD, turn ye even to me with all your heart, and with fasting, and with weeping, and with mourning: and rend your heart, and not your garments, and turn unto the LORD your God: for he is gracious and merciful, slow to anger, and of great kindness, and repenteth him of the evil. Who knoweth if he will return and repent, and leave a blessing behind him; even a meat offering and a drink offering unto the LORD your God?

Blow the trumpet in Zion, sanctify a fast, call a solemn assembly: gather the people, sanctify the congregation, assemble the elders, gather the children, and those that suck the breasts: let the bridegroom go forth of his chamber, and the bride out of her closet (Joel 2:12–16).

The nation that truly turns back to God will know the Lord's hand of judgment lifted from her and will know his bounteous blessing. At the same time, when a nation knows the blessing of God it is the Church's work to call on the nation to bless and praise God for his goodness.

It is certainly true that there is a serious responsibility resting upon the Church's shoulders, but to stand before the nation as God's messenger and prophet is a wonderful privilege. It does not end there though, for we as the Church have also been called to come before the Lord in prayer and supplication on behalf of our own nation in particular, the nation's leaders, and finally the nations in general.

In the course of this book, it has been observed that the acts of a leader can determine whether a nation knows God's blessing or judgment. The reason is because they are representatives of the people. This should lead us to pray fervently for our leaders since what they do will have serious ramifications both in the heavenlies and on the earth. We should not only pray that God would raise up godly leaders, but also that he would cause those in power to submit to his will.

I exhort therefore, that, first of all, supplications, prayers, intercessions, and giving of thanks, be made for all men; for kings, and for all that are in authority; that we may lead a quiet and peaceable life in all godliness and honesty (I Timothy 2:1–2).

Prayer effects mighty things and it is for this reason, if for no other, we should come before the throne of grace seeking mercy and grace for our leaders. True intercession sees godly men and women on their knees petitioning their God to perform miracles and mighty wonders. They pray with clean hands and a pure heart, with a burden given to them from the Lord. The true intercessor, who sees his nation under judgment from God, turns his face to the Lord and cries out for him to remember mercy.

> O LORD, I have heard thy speech, and was afraid: O LORD, revive thy work in the midst of the years, in the midst of the years make known; in wrath remember mercy (Habakkuk 3:2).

As I mentioned in the introduction, I work as an open-air preacher and the subject of suffering comes up on a fairly regular basis. People will ask, 'If there is a God, why is there so much suffering?' The logic of their argument works something along these lines: since there is suffering, God is either too weak to stop it, in which case he isn't God, or he doesn't care, in which case he does not love. Most Christians would probably attempt to answer this conundrum by pointing to the Fall. They would say that God created a perfect world but in due course man disobeyed God and as a result that perfect world was marred. What we see around us does bear testimony to the dreadful effects of sin. However, as we saw previously, it is God who sends the suffering: it was God who cursed the earth, both immediately following Adam's sin and when he sent the Flood. The chaos that afflicted the world, and with it all the suffering that ensued, were not the inevitable consequences of sin, with God there as a passive bystander.

Rather, God saw man's sin and intervened by cursing the earth. It was certainly necessary for God to judge the earth but until he did so the earth was not marred. We have a message that we can take to the unbeliever, that suffering is sent by God. This certainly deals with the problem of God being too weak, since he is the one bringing it about.

However, we are still left with the question, why would a God of love allow or cause people to suffer? As we have seen, 'natural' calamities are God's means of judging the nations with the purpose of bringing them back to him. Rather than pointing to a god who does not care, calamities direct our gaze to God who is intimately involved in his creation and is a righteous Judge. Unregenerate Man, with his self-centred theology, cannot see that everything revolves around God rather than man. Yet the extraordinary thing is that God's judgment has as its purpose the restoration of both the individual and the nation. When the unbeliever asks why there are droughts and storms, we need to answer with true compassion, 'Because he is judging that nation.' We need to point them first to the holiness of God and then to his mercy, which desires that she might return to him in repentance.

Finally, when we understand that God controls all weather at all times we see something of the sovereignty and greatness of God. At the same time we will be brought face to face with our own frailty:

> I have heard of thee by the hearing of the ear: but now mine ear seeth thee. Wherefore I abhor myself, and repent in dust and ashes (Job 42:5–6).

Just as Job was led to worship the Lord in a way he had never done before, so when we come to understand God's power, majesty, and Lordship over all, we bow completely before him.

How small is the Church's vision of God in our day. Our great need is a mighty revelation of God, seated in splendour, Lord over all, righteous in all his ways, judge over all the earth and merciful and gracious to those who seek him.

19

A New Theology

Certainly in previous generations, Christians of all persuasions would have believed that God was the one who controlled the weather. This may be illustrated by the fact that Wesley, Calvin and Matthew Henry all make it clear from their writings that this is what they believed. In Britain this was not confined to Christians, but extended to the unbeliever as well. It is interesting to note that when the Great Storm of 1703 hit the south coast of England many people recognised God's hand of judgment. This was the severest storm England has ever known. About 8,000 lives were lost at sea. In the New Forest alone, 4,000 oak trees were destroyed. In response, the Government of the day called a day of fasting, declaring that the storm 'loudly calls for the deepest and most solemn humiliation of our people.'[69] Similarly, when this nation knew the hand of God's deliverance she gave him praise, as happened following the destruction of the Spanish Armada.

Yet in recent years, as Britain has turned away from God, and in large part come to deny his existence, so the Church has come to deny his Lordship over all things. Few Christians in Britain now acknowledge that God controls the elements. Indeed, large swathes, if not most of the Christian Church in Britain, have absorbed the teaching that the storms, floods and famines that we currently see are the natural consequences of man's treatment of the planet.

Some may argue that this change has come about because of man's increasing knowledge of the scientific world. Yet the word of God has not changed and it makes it plain that it is God who controls the weather.

What has really caused this change in theology? I contend that it stems from a failure to know God. Two aspects of God's nature have largely been ignored. The Church, for the most part, does not believe in the God who is sovereign. Neither does she see God as a righteous Judge. The result has been that she has created a god who is merely here to bless and who only intervenes periodically. She has lost sight of the holiness of God and that he still judges the nations. Consequently, it should not surprise us that there are those in the Church who in recent times have denied the existence of an eternal hell. The god that is being worshipped is not the God of the Bible.

Yet sadly, just as the Church has failed to recognise God in the storm, so she has failed to see him in the rain. When God provides the land with rain so that the crops grow she has not acknowledged the hand of a sovereign merciful God. Rather she sees only the laws of physics in operation. The Church, much like the world, has fixed her eyes on secondary causes rather than the One who is behind it all.

I visited a Church recently which was celebrating 'Environment Sunday'. Little mention was made of the God who is Lord of all. No thanksgiving was given to the One who has blessed Britain year after year with sun and rain that we might have a bountiful harvest. There was no call to repentance, no call to weep before the Lord lest this nation should suffer the same fate as other nations who have suffered God's judgment. Instead we were told to use energy efficient light-bulbs to save the planet. It is God who will bring an end to the planet in his own time because he is Lord.

The Church in Britain has become more concerned with the environment than the winning of souls. Why should I say this? Ask yourself how much time you and your Christian friends spend talking about the environment? How much time do you spend trying to look after the environment, whether it be through recycling or other things? Then think how much it grieves you when you hear about the rainforests being destroyed or other such environmental destruction. Having really considered this, ask yourself how much time you spend in evangelism? How often do you pray for the lost? What we are witnessing in our day is the sin that Jonah was charged with by God himself. He had more pity for a gourd than the souls of thousands which were heading to hell.

> ...The LORD God prepared a gourd, and made it to come up over Jonah, that it might be a shadow over his head, to deliver him from his grief. So Jonah was exceeding glad of the gourd. But God prepared a worm when the morning rose the next day, and it smote the gourd that it withered. And it came to pass, when the sun did arise, that God prepared a vehement east wind; and the sun beat upon the head of Jonah, that he fainted, and wished in himself to die, and said, it is better for me to die than to live. And God said to Jonah, doest thou well to be angry for the gourd? And he said, I do well to be angry, even unto death. Then said the

> LORD, thou hast had pity on the gourd for the which
> thou hast not laboured, neither madest it grow; which
> came up in a night, and perished in a night: and should
> not I spare Nineveh, that great city, wherein are more
> than sixscore thousand persons that cannot discern
> between their right hand and their left hand; and also
> much cattle? (Jonah 4:6–11).

The God of the Bible is sovereign. It is a thread that runs throughout its pages. Yet the truth of it is largely ignored. The words of A. W. Pink are even more applicable to our day than his own:

> That God reigns supreme in heaven, is generally
> conceded; that He does so over this world, is almost
> universally denied – if not directly, then indirectly.
> More and more are men, in their philosophisings and
> theorizings, relegating God to the background. Take
> the material realm. Not only is it denied that God
> created everything, by personal and direct action, but
> few believe that He has any immediate concern in
> regulating the works of His own hands. Everything
> is supposed to be ordered according to impersonal
> and abstract 'laws of Nature.' Thus is the Creator
> banished from His own creation. ...Many suppose that
> He is little more than a far-distant Spectator, taking no
> immediate hand in the affairs of earth. It is true that
> man has a will, but so also has God. It is true that man
> is endowed with power, but God is all-powerful. It
> is true that, speaking generally, the material world is
> regulated by law, but behind that law is the law-Giver
> and law-Administrator.[70]

The believer has lost sight of the supremacy of God over all creation, including over the lives of men and women. Yet is it *really* true that believers today see God as a *far-distant Spectator*? It is certainly true that they cry out to him in their hour of need. However, people now perceive God as merely being there to answer their wishes and commands, rather than the one who is Lord of all. Consider God's message to Jeremiah for the people of Israel, in which he makes it clear that he rules:

> Then the word of the LORD came to me, saying, O house of Israel, cannot I do with you as this potter? saith the LORD. Behold, as the clay is in the potter's hand, so are ye in mine hand, O house of Israel. At what instant I shall speak concerning a nation, and concerning a kingdom, to pluck up, and to pull down, and to destroy it; if that nation, against whom I have pronounced, turn from their evil, I will repent of the evil that I thought to do unto them (Jeremiah 18:5–8).

Rather than seeing ourselves as the clay in the hands of the Potter, Christians have come to view God as the clay. It is as though he may be moulded and made to do that which the people desire. You may think this is blasphemous. That is exactly what it is, yet it is something that has crept into the Church unnoticed. Observe how little is spoken these days of holiness, of submission before God, yet much is spoken of calling on God to bless us. Our prayers are not filled with true humble worship and submission to God's will. Rather they are occupied with our wants. When we suffer, we do not see it as God working out his purposes in our lives: instead we attribute what is happening to the devil. Has Satan usurped God's throne? Has God become subject to the whims of man? The answer is a resounding no.

Returning to A. W. Pink once more, we find the true source of the problem:

> Instead of beginning with man and his world and working back to God, we must begin with God and work down to man – "In the beginning *God*"! Apply this principle to the present situation. Begin with the world as it is today and try to work back to God, and everything will seem to show that God has no connection with the world at all. But begin with God and work down to the world, and light, much light, is cast on the problem. Because God is *holy* His anger burns against sin; because God is *righteous* His judgments fall upon those who rebel against Him; because God is *faithful* the solemn threatenings of His Word are fulfilled; because God is *omnipotent* none can successfully resist Him, still less overthrow His counsel; and because God is *omniscient* no problem can master Him and no difficulty baffle His wisdom. It is just because God is who He is and what He is that we are now beholding on earth what we do – the beginning of His outpoured judgments: in view of His inflexible justice and immaculate holiness we could not expect anything other than what is now spread before our eyes.[71]

The Church has created a man-centred gospel which ignores the sovereignty of God, while at the same time turning God into someone who ignores sin and blesses regardless of our behaviour. The Church, much like the world, has put man at the centre. Holiness and submission to God are no longer required. Instead of our focus being on the Lord who has done wondrous things and demands our obedience, we see only a god who ignores sin and is powerless to intervene in events. Where is the righteous God who shakes the nations and brings to nought those who will exalt themselves against him?

There is a desperate need for the Church once more to seek the face of God. Man must be taken off the throne and God once more must be exalted as King and Lord. This is not limited to our individual lives, but must be acknowledged in all the events that we see unfolding day by day. God is not a bystander, innocently washing his hands of all that happens. He is intimately involved in all things as he fulfils his purposes. God is judge over all the nations and we must acknowledge him as such. There is great security for the believer who does this because he is able to rest in the safe arms of the Lord. It will lead him to walk humbly before the Lord daily. The sovereignty, holiness and justice of God must surely cause us to warn the nations that God will not be mocked and that he still judges the nations. Finally, it should lead us to seek the face of God on behalf of our nation, in the joyful knowledge that God hears the supplications of a broken heart. These are the responses of a people who have recognised God to be both sovereign and judge over all.

Notes

[1] Lloyd-Jones, D. Martyn, *Romans – Exposition of Chapter 8:17–39, The Final Perseverance of the Saints* (The Banner of Truth Trust, Edinburgh, 1987), pp. 50–51, wwwbanneroftruth.co.uk
By permission of The Banner of Truth Trust.

[2] Calvin, John, *Calvin's Commentaries* Volume XIX (Baker Books, Michigan, 1998), p. 165.

[3] Bruce, F. F.; *The Book of the Acts*, (Wm. B. Eerdmans, Michigan, 1995), p. 338.

[4] Job 12:23; Acts 17:26–27.

[5] Lacey, H., *God and the Nations* (John Ritchie Ltd., Scotland, 1991) p.58. By permission of John Ritchie Ltd.

[6] *Matthew Henry's Complete Commentary* on Haggai Chapter 1.

[7] We are given greater insight into what happened in the Letter of James. 'Elias was a man subject to like passions as we are, and he prayed earnestly that it might not rain: and it rained not on the earth by the space of three years and six months. And he prayed again, and the heaven gave rain, and the earth brought forth her fruit' (James 5:17).

[8] *Matthew Henry's Complete Commentary* on II Samuel Chapter 21.

[9] Lacey, H., *God and the Nations* (John Ritchie Ltd., Scotland, 1991) p.113. By permission of John Ritchie Ltd.

[10] Baldwin Smith, Lacey, *The British Empire* (Time-Life Books, 1973), p. 82.

[11] Ibid.; p. 80.

[12] Ibid.; P. 75.

[13] Ibid.; p. 72.

[14] Wesley, John, *Serious Thoughts Occasioned by the Late Earthquake at Lisbon*.

[15] See page 139.

[16] Haining, Peter, *The Great English Earthquake*, (Robert Hale, London, 1991), p.13. Copyright © Peter Haining, 1991. First published in Great Britain by Robert Hale Ltd.

[17] Ibid., pp.17, 19. Copyright © Peter Haining, 1991. First published in Great Britain by Robert Hale Ltd.

[18] Ibid., p. 19. Copyright © Peter Haining, 1991. First published in Great Britain by Robert Hale Ltd.

[19] www.christianaction.org.za, Hammond, Dr. Peter, *Drought, Tsunami's and God*. By permission of Christian Action.

[20] Catholic World News – http://www.cwnews.com/news/viewstory.cfm?recnum=5920
By permission of *Catholic World News*.

[21] http://www.telegraph.co.uk/news/main.jhtml?xml=/news/2002/10/28/nstorm28.xml
By permission of Telegraph Media Group Limited.

[22] *Prophecy Today*, vol. 21, no. 5, September/October 2005, p. 25. By permission of *Sword*

[23] *Prophecy Today*, vol.21, no. 5, September/October 2005, p. 24. By permission of *Sword*

[24] Pearce, T., *Light for the Last Days,* Spring 2001, pp. 12–13. By permission of *Light for the Last Days*.

[25] http://www.opendoorsuk.org/downloads/wwl_downloads/WorldWatchList.pdf

The following countries are the fifty worst offenders, as defined by Open Doors, and are listed in order with the worst offender first.

North Korea, Saudi Arabia, Iran, Somalia, Maldives, Yemen, Bhutan, Vietnam, Laos, Afghanistan, Uzbekistan, China, Eritrea, Turkmenistan, Comoros, Chechnya, Pakistan, Egypt, Myanmar (Burma), North Sudan, Iraq, Azerbaijan, Brunei, Cuba, Qatar, Libya, North Nigeria, Djibouti, India, Sri Lanka, Algeria, Mauritania, Morocco, Tajikistan, Turkey, Oman, Ethiopia, United Arab Emirates, Kuwait, Jordan, Indonesia, Belarus, Colombia (Conflict Areas), Bangladesh, Syria, Tunisia, North East Kenya, Nepal, Mexico, Bahrain.

[26] Prime, Samuel; *The Power of Prayer – The New York Revival of 1858*, (The Banner of Truth Trust, Edinburgh, 1991), p.2, www.banneroftruth.co.uk By permission of The Banner of Truth Trust.

[27] Ibid., p.1. www.banneroftruth.co.uk By permission of The Banner of Truth Trust.

[28] De Young, Donald, *Weather and the Bible*, (Baker Books, Michigan, 1992), pp. 126–127.

[29] New York Times, Weisman, Steven, R., *Japan's Imperial Present*, August 26 1990.

[30] Kovach, R. and McGuire, B., *Philip's Guide to Global Hazards*, (Philip's, London, 2003), p. 66.

[31] *Prophecy Today*, vol. 12, no. 2, March/April 1996, *The Shaking of Japan* by Jerome Mouat. By permission of *Sword*.

[32] Yohannan, K. P., *Revolution in World Missions*, (gfa books, USA 2004) , pp. 137–138. By permission of Gospel for Asia.

[33] Lancaster, J., *Outracing The Sea, Orphans in His Care*, *Washington Post* Foreign Service, Thursday, December 30, 2004.

[34] De Young, Donald, *Weather and the Bible*, (Baker Books, Michigan, 1992), p. 85.

[35] Ibid, p.86.

[36] Gardner, D., *The Trumpet Sounds for Britain*, Vol. II, (Jesus is Alive! Ministries, Southend-on-Sea, 2002), pp. 49–51. By permission of Jesus is Alive! Ministries.

[37] Ibid., p.118. By permission of Jesus is Alive! Ministries.

[38] http://news.bbc.co.uk/1/hi/world/africa/300648.stm

[39] http://www.globalconnections.co.uk/beinformed/worldstories/Africa/Diviner.htm By permission of Aim International.

[40] www.jesus.org.uk/dawn/1999/dawn9916.html By permission of OMF International. Copyright © OMF International www.omf.org

[41] *Prophecy Today*, vol. 20, no.2, March/April 2004, p. 24. By permission of *Sword*.

[42] Lee, Laura, *Blame it on the Rain*, (HarperCollins, New York, 2006), p. 256.

[43] Ibid., p. 114.

[44] *The Forsaken Promise* (Hatikvah Film Trust, 2004) DVD. By permission of Hatikvah Film Trust.

[45] *Prophecy Today*, vol. 19, no.1, January/February 2003, p.30. By permission of *Sword*.

[46] http://visibleearth.nasa.gov/view_rec.php?vev1id=5989 By permission NASA.

[47] Koenig, W., *Eye to Eye*, (About Him Publishing, Alexandria, 2006), pp.40–41. By permission of About Him Publishing.

[48] Ibid., p.42. By permission of About Him Publishing.

[49] Ibid., p. 153. By permission of About Him Publishing.

[50] Ibid., pp. 155–156. By permission of About Him Publishing.

[51] http://news.bbc.co.uk/1/hi/england/london/6217514.stm

[52] http://www.timesonline.co.uk/tol/news/world/middle_east/ article1294196.ece By permission of Times Newspapers Ltd.

[53] http://www.timesonline.co.uk/tol/news/world/middle_east/ article1294196.ece By permission of Times Newspapers Ltd.

[54] http://news.independent.co.uk/world/americas/article2214846. ece; Unborne, D., *Curfew in Florida after storms leave 20 dead*, 4th February 2007. By permission of Independent News & Media plc.

[55] The king's heart is in the hand of the LORD, as the rivers of water: he turneth it whithersoever he will (Proverbs 21:1).

[56] Wilkerson, D., *Hungry for More of Jesus*, (Rickfords Hill Publishing Ltd., Aylesbury, 2003), p.46.
By permission of Rickfords Hill Publishing Ltd.

[57] http://www.epa.gov/climatechange/basicinfo.html

[58] Alexander, J., Sophie Harding, *For Tomorrow Too; Living Responsibly in a world of climate change*, (Tearfund, 2006, Second Edition). Copyright © *Tearfund UK 2008. (www.tearfund.org)*

[59] Ibid., p. 7. Copyright © *Tearfund UK 2008. (www.tearfund.org)*

[60] The report referred to was published in August 2006 in the journal *Global Change Biology*.

[61] Maslin, M., *Global Warming, A Very Short Introduction*, (OUP, Oxford, 2004), pp. 57–58. By permission of Oxford University Press.

[62] http://www.answersingenesis.org/creation/v17/i4/ conservation.asp; *Creation and Conservation* by Ken Ham. By permission of Answers in Genesis.

[63] De Young, Donald; *Weather and the Bible*, (Baker Books, Michigan, 1992), pp. 133–134.

[64] http://nov55.com/gbwg.html

⁶⁵ http://www.telegraph.co.uk/news/worldnews/1542332/
Cosmic-rays-blamed-for-global-warming.html
By permission of The Telegraph Media Group Limited.
⁶⁶ Calder, N., *The Chilling Stars*, (Icon books, Cambridge, 2007),
pp.79-81
⁶⁷ http://larouchepac.com/news/2008/02/28/atmospheric-co2-its-
oceans-stupid.html Article by Professor Endersbee.
By permission of 21st Century Science & Technology
⁶⁸ The two discourses in Matthew and Luke, though related, are
very different in their content. The reason for this is that in Luke
we find Jesus primarily concerned with when the temple will
be destroyed, while in Matthew, Jesus deals with the end of the
age. This may be seen by comparing the way each deals with
the persecution of believers.

In Luke, Jesus speaks of a persecution taking place before the
calamities (Luke 21:10-12). There is also a significant period of
time between the two, since the persecution runs until the times
of the Gentiles are fulfilled (Luke 21:24-25). The discourse in
Luke fits perfectly with the events of AD 70 (Luke 21:20-24), and
therefore we can say that there will be a length of time between
AD 70 and the calamities described. This is where Matthew
picks things up. He has the calamities followed by another time
of persecution (Matthew 24:6-9, 29-30) which will immediately
precede the end of the age.

Both Matthew and Luke speak of persecution but they are
referring to different occasions separated by a significant period
of time. Both Matthew and Luke set the calamities in the context
of the end of the age.
⁶⁹ http://www.uab.edu/english/hone/etexts/edb/day-pages/331-
nov27.html

[70] Pink, A. W., *The Sovereignty of God*, (The Banner of Truth Trust, Edinburgh, 1972), pp.12, 16, www.banneroftruth.co.uk

By permission of The Banner of Truth Trust.

[71] Ibid., p.17. www.banneroftruth.co.uk

By permission of The Banner of Truth Trust.

For more great Christian books, including our
One Pound Classics series, please visit our
website at www.rhpbooks.co.uk, or send a large
stamped and addressed envelope to RHP,
PO Box 576, Aylesbury, HP22 6XX